practice
of consumption
and spaces
for goods

francesca murialdo

ABSTRACT

The change in the significance of goods is a process which has triggered far-reaching changes in society as the term has lost any meaning in relation to its purely functional character and increasingly come to represent symbolic and cultural contents.

The practice of consumption seems today to be one of the distinctive features by means of which we can describe the social, political and economic phenomenologies which, for better or worse, influence our lives.

What becomes increasingly evident and necessary is the role of design culture as a structure for the coordination of the networks of knowledge, to interpret the world of things and design in order to influence behaviours, in the final analysis, bringing about the rise of new economies.

The practice of consumption and the spaces for goods are in continuous evolution, constantly eluding typological and functional definition. One of the objectives of this research, besides an attempt to explore not only the spaces but also the practices of consumption from the designer's perspective, is to understand what mechanisms are at work, what competences, the roles which have impacted on, still impact on today and will continue to impact on this sector in the future.

INDEX

0
foreword

practice of consumption and spaces for goods

The idea of concentrating on Retail as a specific field of research, paradigmatic for the considerable transformations occurred in the interior discipline, both for investigation and criticism, started few years ago with my PhD thesis (a special thanks to professors Luciano Crespi, Politecnico di Milano, Louise Crewe, University of Nottingham, Christoph Grafe, TU Delft, Francesco Scullica, Politecnico di Milano); since then I've been involved in research, professional practice, academic and teaching activity, met a lot of people involved in various aspects of the *retail* area.

I finally decided to publish part of my considerations in this essay to set a start for a thinking over and to meet the lack of writings on the topic.

From a formal point of view, it would have been too much demanding to collect all the authorizations to publish the pictures in consideration that we have plenty of wonderful pictures on many books on the market and on the web; in the e-book and in the printable version we then decided to insert some link to give the chance to the reader to make also visual connection: in the text flow you'll find a hyperlink or a QR-Code with a very short description of its content in the following form

>>name, name

Where possible we've tried to link directly to the designer page but sometimes we discovered beautiful images in various independent blogs.

Retail, set on the spaces characterized by the selling of goods, it's the place favoured by experimental innovation both on formal and typological point of view. From one side is a project field quite new, been snobbed for few decades from the designer's side but, on the other hand, is the engine of the globalized world economy, that reflects not only habits and forms of the contemporary society, but also involves thinking about places and methods of the production of goods in the vision of the new consumption geography.

The change in the significance of goods is a process which, ever since the end of the Industrial Revolution, has triggered far-reaching changes in society as the term has lost any meaning in relation to its purely functional character and increasingly come to represent symbolic and cultural contents.

The practice of consumption seems today to be one of the distinctive features by means of which we can describe the social, political and economic phenomenologies which, for better or worse, influence our lives.

This radical transformation has led to the creation of specialised, refined, «ideologically informed» places, as Tony Fretton[1] defines them: from *passages* to *concept stores*, these special places occupy an increasingly central role in society and in the organization of our landscape; nodal nerve centres which concentrate around themselves and absorb spaces dedicated to entertainment, culture and socializing.

---

[1] Vernet, D., de Wit, L., *Boutiques and Other Retail Spaces*, Routledge, New York 2007, Foreword.

1| Theran, the Bazaar

It is clear that a radical change is taking place in the behavior of companies, in the needs of the clients, the typologies of goods, the role of the retail outlet, and in design tools. The shop today is no longer at the end of a process of giving meaning to a brand, but is rather at the centre of this production process and the cause of a continually changing panorama.

Typology is not being transformed but disappearing, new forms arise with such diverse presuppositions as to generate new spaces with new contents and new meanings.

Interior design, which is intimately interconnected with technological innovation, marketing, management, psychology, and sociology, plays a decisive role, while a more widespread planning quality into existence entrusted to the consumers themselves.

How will the places of commerce-consumption be transformed in the future?

What sort of evolution will there be in the contamination between places and activities?

What role will shopping play in the global economy?

Will it still make any sense to define these places in terms of typology or will they be so different from themselves as to merit other definitions?

What role will architecture and interior design play in the design of the places of consumption in the design culture?

The invasion of our landscape by commercial containers on different scales, the sudden interest in the design of these places which had for so long been relegated by design culture to a secondary role, correspond to the appearance on bookshop shelves of a vast number of glossy publications which bear witness to the enormous investment, both economic and cultural, which has been made in these places over the past two decades.

The practice of consumption and the spaces of goods are in continuous evolution, constantly eluding typological and functional definition. One of the objectives of this research, besides an attempt to explore not only

practice of consumption and spaces for goods

the spaces but also the practices of consumption from the designer's perspective, is to understand what mechanisms are at work, what competences, the roles which have impacted on, still impact on today and will continue to impact on this sector in the future. In recent years there has been talk of *Retail Design* as if it were a discipline apart[2], a sub-sector of what is known as *Experience Design* and which refers in a much more general manner to an approach, a methodology, a complex compendium which touches on diverse disciplines with the ultimate objective of concentrating on the satisfaction of the client in relation to the experience of purchasing. Design, in the traditional sense of the word, comes into play within a complex network of disciplines which support one another in the production of a three-dimensional physical design.

In her book, Marina Fumo wonders whether «the places and architectures of commerce change with society and follow the transformations in it or whether it is the laws of the market which propose new models which induce the consumer to buy more?»[3].

The answer seems to be a combination of both hypotheses and we must ask ourselves how the role of the designer and of the discipline itself has changed over recent years.

The hypothesis is that the interiors discipline occupies a fundamental role, that of an interface, and the discipline which encapsulates the contributions of others, specifically assimilates instruments and methods of enquiry to then translate the new requirements into physical places in relation to the consumer, the user, the person. The final interface, the shop, outlet, shopping centre, independently of its typology, becomes the litmus paper for verification, subsequent analysis, the re-introduction of the other disciplines which study it in order to identify

---

[2] Kindleysides, J., *Retail design*, Design Council, http://www.designcouncil.org.uk, Ardill, R., *Experience design*, Design Council, http://www.designcouncil.org.uk.

[3] Fumo, M., curated by, *Dal mercato ambulante all'outlet. Luoghi e architetture per il commercio*, Editrice Compositori, Bologna 2004, p. 158.

further requirements and provide a subsequent brief for a subsequent manipulation of the space.

The central role which certain disciplines have played in the prefiguration of the organization of commercial spaces, suffice to mention the omnipresence of *experience marketing*, seems to allow space for more refined and differentiated studies, more circumscribed and less absolutist reflection with reference to small groups of consumers, individuals who, having been transformed from citizens into consumers, seem capable of once again assuming a primary role which can exert an influence on global economies. The order of things seems to have been turned on its head, if before, it was the requirements of production, distribution and sales of the companies which influenced typologies of consumption (*consume-centred*)[4], today it is social phenomena which influence company planning (*consumer-centred*)[5].

> «People are increasingly informed, independent minded and aesthetically sophisticated so brands have to generate a cultural relevant dialogue within their costumer communities and show in every communication effort that they bring genuine added value»[6].

This study is motivated by the consideration that it is necessary to enquire into the series of meaningful transformations which have affected both commercial spaces and consumption practices, which have major consequences on the organization of our day to day life as well as on the shape of our cities.

The essay is subdivided into three sections: *The practice of consumption*, *The spaces of goods* and *Findings: Pointers and Hypotheses*.

The first section is a transversal reading of the phenomenology of

---

[4] In Italy an enterprise as Fiat had a very strong appeal in the social and landscape transformations; one of the strongest motivating force for the construction of the highway system in the Fifties has been the necessity to sell cars.

[5] Many enterprises adopt in their goals the resources preservation because it's requested by the society (Ikea, Body Shop, Lush, and others).

[6] Johnston, L., Agneessens, S., "The Culture of Commerce", *GDR Creative Review*, n. 26, September 2007.

practice of consumption and spaces for goods

design of consumption spaces, a critical reading of the processes currently under way which aims to identify the dynamics of change. As well as providing an analysis of the typologies of certain spaces for commerce, there is a comparison of some contemporary phenomena in the spheres of politics, economics and society, with designs of places of consumption providing a map of themes which in the near future will see radical changes.

The second section aims to act as a bridge between the first and third chapters: the hypothesis of interpretation set out in the first section and the *Pointers/Hypotheses* in the third are filtered through an analysis of some paradigmatic designs by some of the most influential designers of the 20th and 21st centuries. *Progenitors* of schools of thought, innovators, people who could still even now inspire us to come up with new design strategies.

The third is an open chapter where we pose questions while examining a series of pointers which might provide us with the tools to formulate hypotheses about future models in the field of design of spaces for commerce.

The continuous thread which runs through the study is determined by the need to look *from the inside* the processes which bring about changes, put these in relationship with the city, society and its individual inhabitants. The retail outlet is a place in which there is a concentration and overlap of forms of expression and communication of various kinds. It is not therefore a mere physical space, the result of architectural design, but it is the terminus of a complex system of variables correlated to as many different disciplines. What emerges as increasingly fundamental is the central role of design which must analyse and provide solutions capable of interpreting these new requirements.

1
practice
of consumption

1.1

introduction

practice of consumption and spaces for goods

«Some think that buying things that you don't "need" is immoral, but all of us do it»[1] was the controversial statement of Kevin Ervin Kelley from the pages of the Harvard Design Magazine against those who insisted on seeing the sphere of consumption as the malevolent part of capitalist society. Throughout history, places of commerce have been among the privileged places in which social, economic and political needs have been discussed and implemented which transformed the modern world. The role, organisation and form of these places are both mirror and precursor to the changes in society. The shop (or any other form of space for commerce) cannot be simply reduced to its physical appearance but its *form* is the result of a combination of economic, social and material factors, and the task of the designer is to act as a mediator and interpreter

---

[1] Kelley, K. E., "Architecture for Sale(s)", *Harvard Design Magazine*, n. 17, Fall 2002 Winter 2003.

of an increasingly complex set of needs.

Although the history of commerce and the organisation of its spaces has always been marked by continuous innovation, in recent years we have seen a dramatic increase in design in this context, so that design of commercial space has come to be a specific and autonomous discipline in its own right, what is increasingly referred to as *Retail Design*.

This section aims to highlight the connections between the practice of consumption, the mechanisms regulating it and the players involved, while the section *The spaces of commerce*, will examine these ideas within the context of disciplinary debate.

>>Hermes, Prassitele, IV century a.C., Archeological Museum, Olympia. Mercurio, or Hermes, it's the god of oratory, commerce, robbers and doctors

The history of retail is the history of society, its rules and relationships. Adolf Loos' shop Knitže is as inviting as it is clearly exclusive and intended for a social class with the economic capability to pay for the prestigious garments for sale. Department Stores on the other hand were designed for the middle class which, for the first time, began to see shopping as a leisure activity, and could avail of services which until that moment were the only prerogative of the elite.

The dominant models of the shop or the shopping centre reflect two different societies. One is that which lives in the city, in the historic centre, organised on the basis of a functional hierarchy, and characterised by clearly defined areas and recognisable elements. This contrasts with the suburbs, programmatically fleeing from the model of the historic city centre, responding to a democratic non-differentiation of spaces, well represented by the organisation of shopping centres where there is consolation in the economic homogeneity and the underlying understanding of an affinity of intentions.

These different societies with their different organisational structures influence the form of spaces and their meaning, attributing different cultural contents to each individual element. Whereas, in the United States, the profession of the small shopkeeper received no great social recognition, so much so that it was the preserve of immigrants and outsiders, in Europe, the merchant has always enjoyed an undisputed social respectability. In the United States, the shopping centres are the expression of the alternative to the city, monuments erected at that time when Americans turned their backs on the city, islands, not easy to reach by public transport. Conversely, in Japan, they are always well connected by public transport and are found in nodal areas in urban connections.

>>The Passage, St. Petersburg, 1902

As Bourdieu[2] states in his study of modern taste, economic and social capital frequently define one another by opposition: it is necessary to overcome this dualism in order to explore the diverse ways in which aspects of cultural production are influenced by the economic environment. Even that which seems merely a result of market requirements dictated by rational calculations of an economic nature is rooted in cultural processes. A parallel analysis of culture and economics, exploring the relationship between production and consumption, opens the way for a new perspective from which to interpret contemporary phenomena.

«the economy is increasingly culturally inflected and [...] culture is more and more economically inflected»[3].

[2] Bourdieu, P., *Distinction: A Social Critique of the Judgement of Taste*, Routledge & Kegan Paul, London 1984.

[3] Lash, S., Urry, J., *Economies of Signs and Space*, Sage, London 1994, p. 64.

It is to Bourdieu too that we owe the insight that consumption, through its actors, should be considered as an independent field of research, completely separate from production issues, and tending towards comparative study with other theoretical frameworks. From psychoanalysis to social constructivism, the consumer objects become key elements for the construction of the self and identity, above all for sexual and ethnic identity, while consumption is starting to be recognised as one of the keys for interpretation of modernity.

The places of consumption are no longer seen as *passive* but as spaces with specific properties which can come into play in the construction of difference.

2| Liberty' stall, a location for 100% Design, London 2009

Even prestigious brand as the Londoner Liberty, characterized by an image linked to the historical shop in London's Regent' Street, doesn't give up selling occasions even if has to disregard its image, here just represented by the shopping bags in a way decorating the stall

1.2

«todo se ha vuelto tiendas»

practice of consumption and spaces for goods

The history of spaces for commerce can be told by means of the typological innovations, the use of innovative materials and technologies, or tied in with events which have made a significant impression on the course of history.

As early as 1606, Lope de Vega[1] describing Madrid as the new capital, underlined how dominant the role of commercial spaces had become. In brief, it can be said that the architecture of commercial spaces developed from two typological elements, the shop and the market stall.

The market was not only one of the focal points around which the social life of the city was organised, but was also an organising element of the form of the city, with the stereometric module of the stall, modular, which has been passed on over the years, practically unchanged, to modern

---

[1] «Everything has been transformed into shops»: in 1606 Lope de Vega describes Madrid just became capital, in Braudel, F. *I giochi dello scambio*, Torino 1981, p. 43.

times. The shop on the other hand, not visible in the finger print of the city has undergone a series of evolutions both from the technological and symbolic viewpoints. These reflect, and at times anticipate, some of the most important developments in society.

Two elements have been responsible for introducing profound changes to every aspect of European culture at the end of the 18th century: the French Revolution and the Industrial Revolution.

The French Revolution introduced laws on the free market with the elimination of the obligation on shopkeepers to be members of strict guilds. Up until that moment, it had been the guilds that organised the shops, concentrating them in particular districts. Now shopkeepers were free to choose where to set up shop, trying out different types of collaboration with other shopkeepers. This was the origin of the *passages*: the first example was the Galerie de Bois, a temporary wooden structure built in 1786 behind the Palais Royal in Paris[2].Its success was such that it was then built in a permanent form in 1829. The *passages*, or *arcades* in their English version, proved to be perfect places for commerce, a public space where one could spend time and find products and entertainment under the same roof. The typology of *arcades*, and *passages*, set in motion a mechanism which would create a lasting connection between the practice of consumption and other entertainment activities. Apart from shops, the *passage* in Nevskij Prospekt in St. Petersburg in 1850 contained bars, pastry shops, an anatomy museum, a waxworks and even a small zoo[3].

The Industrial Revolution, which spread from England all over Europe from the mid-18th century, introduced radical changes in the cycle of production and distribution of goods and services. Faster production, the

---

[2] Cfr. Pevsner brings back the source of the *passages* and of the *arcades* to the Royal Exchange founded in London in 1565 by Thomas Gresham. It was possible there to hire spaces for craftsman and merchants in Pevsner, N., *A History of Building Types*, Princeton Architectural Press, New York 1976, trad. it. *Storia e caratteri degli edifici*, Fratelli Palombi Editori, Roma 1986, p. 317.

[3] Cfr. Benjamin,W., *Das Passagen-Werk*, Suhrkamp, Frankfurt a. M. 1982, trad. it., *Paris, capitale del XIX secolo. I passages di Paris*, Einaudi, Torino 1986. In particular *Passages, magasins de nouveauté(s), calicots*, p. 41, *Il flâneur* p. 465.

practice of consumption and spaces for goods

development of rail transport and the steam engine for the production of work tools, introduced radical changes within the world of commerce. From a typological viewpoint, for the first time there came to be a clear separation between the public areas and the home of the shopkeeper, between the production area and the sales area, spaces which had often overlapped in previous spatial types. There was a progression from the *shop* model, where goods were sold alongside the workshops where they were produced, to that of the *store*[4], where products were kept in another place altogether, the precursor of the new model of the *department stores*.

Technology applied to spaces for commerce had two fundamental objectives up until the 19th century: to make more efficient use of surfaces (in order to display a greater number of goods) and to improve communications between the exterior and interior of the retail space. Construction methods and materials played, and continue to play, a decisive role in marking these evolutionary steps. Just think of how glass and the escalator innovated and modified the organisation of retail interiors. The first shops with transparent display windows appeared in Holland at the start of the 19th century and became common in Europe around 1850[5]: this not only marked the introduction of the fundamental element of communication between the exterior and interior, but also made it possible to have a deeper space (from the facade inwards) now that the sunlight could penetrate further. From the end of the 18th century, experimentation with iron structures led to the crucial definition of the open floor. Among other advantages, it was now possible to unite two adjacent units, and for the first time differentiate between the size of spaces which led to the development of different types of sales. Subsequently, the escalator was the technological innovation which made it possible to exploit sales spaces above the ground floor, leading

---

[4] Both *shop* and *store* are translated in italian with *negozio*; actually *shop* is *negozio* and *store* should be *magazzino*, in italian just used in the meaning of *grande magazzino*.

[5] Pevsner, N., *A History of Building Types*, Princeton Architectural Press, New York 1976, trad. it. *Storia e caratteri degli edifici*, Fratelli Palombi Editori, Roma 1986.

to the development of *department stores*.

>>Frantz Jourdain, facade of the La Samaritaine, Paris 1907
La Samaritaine opens in 1867, just after Bon Marché in 1852, considered to be the first department store. In 1905 it has been transformed by Frantz Jourdain, friend of Émile Zola. Today's facade it's been designed by Sauvage in 1927. La Samaritaine it's one of the main character of the famous novel by Émile Zola, *Au Bonheur des Dames* dated 1883.

At the turn of the 20th century, in the Golden Age of Art Nouveau, the facades of commercial spaces and their interiors were richly decorated, bearing witness to the symbolic value of these buildings in the architectural culture of the period.

Modernism, while relegating commerce to the margins in favour of other themes considered to be more ethical[6], proved a fundamental period for the appearance in France of the first publications written and illustrated by architects dealing with the subject of shops: *Devantures de boutique* by Sèzille[7] published in 1927, used illustrations to show projects which had already been built, and in 1931 *Boutique*[8] by Roger Poulain used photographs to illustrate contemporary interiors and decor.

It would not be until the end of the Second World War that another typological revolution would take place, dictated this time by the mass market and the introduction of new consumer credit instruments (loans and mortgages) which, apart from stimulating the economic recovery, generated new needs which the market aimed to meet. Consumer society, created by economic policy in the United States, became a global phenomenon and the market became the greatest political power[9].

---

[6] The Athens Charter dated 1933, manifest of the Modern Movement, identifies the design culture through the four functions of *dwelling, work, recreation* and *transport*, excluding *commerce* from the functional map of the Modern City.

[7] Sézille, L.P., *Devantures de Boutique*, Editions Albert Lévy, Paris 1927.

[8] Poulain, R., *Boutiques* 1931, Paris 1931.

[9] in Europe the Marshall Plan (1947) for reconstruction, finance and develops a consumer's society on the model of the american one.
According the International Council of Shopping Centers the selling volume of Wal-Mart (Wal-Mart is an American multinational retail corporation) is bigger than the gross national product of three quarters of the world national economies (in C. J. Chung, J. Inaba, R. Koolhaas, S. T. Leong, *Harward Design School Guide to Shopping*, Taschen, Köln 200, p. 67).

practice of consumption and spaces for goods

The importance that was given to the private sphere and hard won freedom was underlined by the marketing of household appliances and the mobility which were to become paradigms of the modern lifestyle. Once these essential needs had been satisfied, consumer attitudes became increasingly refined and themselves gave rise to more complex and significant places.

>>The cover of Boutiques 1931

3| Detail of Il Buon Governo in città, Ambrogio Lorenzetti, 1338-39

1.2.1

THE SHOP

«The evolution of shop design was very slow. There is no substantial difference between the shops in the Trajan forum (early 2nd century B.C.) or in Ostia (mid-2nd century A.D.) and the shop painted by Ambrogio Lorenzetti in 1338-39 in his fresco of "Buon Governo in città"»[1]

The shop changes shape, dimensions and adapts to the new spaces of commerce. In Department Stores, the shop becomes a stall, kiosk, corner, shop-in-shop, showing a great flexibility which makes any typological definition difficult.
The small specialised shop, the *specialty shop*, which offered the customer something exclusive basing the sales transaction on a relationship of trust between the shopkeeper and customer suffered under the conditions of modernity. The decontextualisation of the small local shop, which based its relationship on proximity, moved to planned shopping areas, the *high street* and *shopping malls,* now became inadequate and had to adopt new sales strategies, turning into something other than what it originally was.

>>The house di Raffaello, Bramante, 1514

>>The Bakery Shop, Job Berckheyde, 1680

---

[1] Pevsner, N., *A History of Building Types*, Princeton Architectural Press, New York 1976, trad. it. *Storia e caratteri degli edifici*, Fratelli Palombi Editori, Roma 1986, p. 311.
Till when the domestic and commercial activities were promiscuous, the shop, the space voted to relate to the public, was defined by the counter that was the border in between inside (private) and outside (public). With the separation of the two functions (commercial and domestic), space got bigger, the shop opens its doors and the counter moves in a position perpendicular to the entrance facade.

The baby boom of the Post-war period gave a great impetus to the retail sector and brought about rapid changes in the nature of the individual shop. The concept of chain store introduced substantial changes to the form, management and meaning of the shop. Distribution meant that it was no longer necessary to devote space to store rooms. The role of the owner-shopkeeper disappeared and the bond of trust between product and customer was handed over to advertising. The emphasis shifted from the product to the shop image which turned into a concept.

1,242,872.
SELF SERVING STORE.

4| Drawing of a self-service store

The 1980s saw the consolidation of the idea of the shop as a necessary complement to the product, while during the 90s, the physical space of the shop increasingly became a privileged place of representation of the product. The retail outlet was transformed by marketing into a consumer experience space where shopping is mixed with other forms of entertainment.

«These are not the temples of shopping but rather temples of entertainment»[2], says Stefano Casciani. From this moment forward, the typological definition shop no longer suffices as the retail space is subdivided into its contemporary forms of concept store, flagship store, temporary shop, corner...

>>Walker Evans Seed Store 1936, interior
The relationship with the next door shop, that was able to offer a great quantity of goods, was created by the owner, a person able to give advices for good clients. This figure disappears with chain stores. The typology of the shop is no more linked to the typology of the goods and assumes new contents.

[2] Casciani, S. "La moda, lo stile e il mercato", *Domus*, n. 833, p. 42.

5| Beijing, 2009

1.2.2

SHOP OF SHOPS

«the house must become a cathedral of commerce for a people of customers, a department store of functional architecture [...] make a poem of modern activity through the life of a department store»[1].

The *department store* was the first true urban phenomenon. It was one of the most innovative places which had the greatest influence on the market place from the mid-19th century until around 1930.
The first department store was opened by Aristide Boucicaut in Paris[2]: Bon Marché, the small shop opened in 1838, contained a huge range of consumer goods inside a single building. For the first time, prices were fixed and there were policies set for changing goods or refund.

>>Au Bon Marchè, Charles Boileau and
Gustave Eiffel, 1880

>>Au Bon Marchè, 1880

The influence of this new type of retail space had an enormous impact

---

[1] Zola, E., *Au Bonheur des dames*, s.e., Paris 1883, trad it. *Al paradiso delle signore*, Rizzoli, Milano 1959.

[2] The typology of the department store has been foreseen by the opening of the *magasins de nouveautés* in France, in the second half of XVIII century, in Pevsner, N., *A History of Building Types*, Princeton Architectural Press, New York 1976, trad. it. *Storia e caratteri degli edifici*, Fratelli Palombi Editori, Roma 1986.

not only on the economy but on society and daily routine which, from this moment onwards, would undergo an irreversible transformation. This marked the rise of consumer culture which would open the way some decades in the future for the shopping mall. As has already been stressed above, some technological innovations such as the escalator and gas lighting were determining factors for not only the development but even for the very concept of this new type.

Vertical development was the impetus for research into new technologies and materials like glass, heating and air conditioning systems, lighting systems. Even the layout of the new retail spaces was influenced by a new focus on the study of paths and the attitudes of the new consumers. From the very outset, and for the first time, retail business went side by side with some other services such as restaurants, bathroom facilities, and reading rooms, which had the precise objective of increasing the amount of time a customer spent in the retail outlet in the conviction that this would therefore increase his desire to buy.

From the point of view of social structure, the department store plays a fundamental role in the emancipation of women. From the viewpoint of consumer practices, for the first time it became morally acceptable that women go shopping alone. From the point of view of employment, the department store offered women work opportunities with a high level of professionalism.

But the most striking element of the phenomenon remains the rise of a new consumer ethics which in this period clearly represents the success of the American economic system.

The department store was also instrumental in the production and consequent distribution of mass-produced products: clothes manufactured using new industrial facilities and small domestic appliances.

The fate of the department store is indissolubly linked with urban life: its success is linked to the development of the city and its decline to the move of the inhabitants of the city to the suburbs.

The aspect of democratisation of consumption whereby the same retail outlet could equally serve people of different status belonging to different social classes, was another reason for its success and decline from the mid-20th century onwards. The city, no longer welcoming to all but elitist, banished part of the population to the suburbs, thus decreeing the downfall of that form of commerce which had been generated by the city itself.

The *shopping centre*, or *commercial mall*[3], came into being in the United States following the rapid development of residential suburbs, the spread of car ownership and the possibility of buying cheap land. Its history and its development is quite different from that of the department store. The architectural attention that the department store had managed to attract, the presentation of the goods starting with the packaging of the building itself which occupied a prominent position in the historic centre of the city, all of this was abandoned completely with the mall.

Seen from the outside, the mall is what has been called a *big box*: a series of big containers, one after the other, without any breaks in an out-of-town landscape with no aesthetic or functional connotations.

The very idea of the *mall*, the first example of which was built about 70 years ago in Edina in Minnesota[4], is the way in which the structure is presented which reflects the management of the space.

The spaces devoted to commerce have always been organised and managed by the merchants themselves who, in order to attract customers, made certain to provide pleasant places, exotic goods and attention to the finest detail, beginning with the bazaar where each little shop is an expression and property of a different shopkeeper. This tradition, as we have seen, is a common thread among all the places of commerce, from the tiny space of the streetseller in an open-air market to the large department store which, even today, conserves much of its charm thanks to this very architectural tradition and decorated both the interior and

---

[3] *Shopping Mall* loan its name from *The Mall*, the walk in St. James in London where people used to go to have a rest at the end of the working day.

[4] Many sources agree on Southdale in Edina, opened in 1956, to be the first shopping mall in history. Pevsner instead quotes the first one to be Lijnbaan in Rotterdam, designed by Johannes H. van der Broek e Jacob B. Bakema, in Pevsner, N., *A History of Building Types*, Princeton Architectural Press, New York 1976, trad. it. *Storia e caratteri degli edifici*, Fratelli Palombi Editori, Roma 1986.

exterior space (an example of this would be Macey's in new York or La Rinascente in Milan).

>>Macy's Entrance, 34th Street, New York

Whereas the architecture of the department stores has deep roots in the culture of modern architecture (Eiffel, for example, was involved in the design of Bon Marché), the owners of these shops were men who proudly called the shops, an expression of their own personality and ambition, by their own name (Macey, Wanamaker, Gimbel, Neiman, Marcus, Marshallfield,...).

Malls play host to sales outlets but neither belong to nor were thought up by shopkeepers. Their image is subject to the rules of the big real estate agents which rent out the spaces and take a percentage of the earnings, without worrying overmuch about the impact on the territory. When the malls are urban, we have some examples, above and beyond a critical or architectural judgement, of how this typology can acquire some sort of design dignity. It is often the municipal authorities that impose some sort of aesthetic values on them and, added to the content, this is often expedient for the redevelopment and renewal of problem areas. In recent years, in the United States, in the face of a dramatic fall in population, the mall industry has entered an irreversible recession. These containers devoid of any symbolic connotation become difficult to put back on the market.

The crisis of the shopping centre model on the other side of the Atlantic means that the *fantasy palace*, traditionally associated with the «phantasmagoria of objects and goods», in the words of Walter Benjamin[5], no longer occupies the privileged role of favourite place to

----

[5] Benjamin, W., *Das Passagen-Werk*, Suhrkamp, Frankfurt a. M. 1982, trad. it., *Paris, capitale del XIX secolo. I passages di Paris*, Einaudi, Torino 1986.

practice of consumption and spaces for goods

get away from it all of the 21st century consumer[6]. If the malls close down, the retail space is taken over by some other formulas, in part directly deriving from the mall, in part a reinterpretation of older forms, and in part by entirely new concepts.

The Natural Shopping Centres, so defined as distinct from those constructed artificially or rather constructed by means of artifice, are «the streets, squares, arcades, historic centres and quarters in which shops, craft workshops, bars, restaurants and facilities have tended to concentrate in a spontaneous manner throughout the course of history», as Rosario Cardillo[7] points out. The transformation of spontaneity into an organised system, an operation *a posteriori*, a reorganisation of the preexisting with an added emphasis on the theme of commerce, already in existence in the consolidated urban fabric. The limit of this operation seems to lie in the type of the intervention which seems to fizzle out into the fields of street furniture or communication design.

>>Maremagnum, Old Port, Barcelona
As other parts of the city even the Old Port has been strongly modified during re-convertion works held in occasion of the Olympic Games in 1992. Home of fishermen and fish markets has been transformed in one of the main leisure centres of Barcelona: shopping centres, restaurants, and cinemas. The newest area is occupied by Maremagnum, a big shopping centre with bars, fast foods and leisure attractions.

>>Atlantic Station, Atlanta
In Atlanta a former industrial area has been converted in mix-use commercial, residential and entertainment spaces.

To remain with large scale retail, recent years have seen the arrival of a phenomenon which has met with huge success, the Retail Park, which

---

[6] «The average time shoppers spent in malls dropped by half from 1980 to 1990» in Hassell, G., "Malls slipping as Shopping meccas", *Houston Cronicle*, 9th October 1996, n.1.
«Vacant big box space in the Chicago area now totals more than 12 millions square feet» in Handley, J., "Big boxes not always the best gift", *Chicago Tribune*, 24 December, 1995.

[7] In the public competition *Astambein Scenografie urbane per le Terre dell'Unione*, design competition.

in Italy generally goes under the name of Outlet, enormous thematic open air malls[8]. These new structures are no longer the place of the surreal, *fantasy palaces*, but on the opposite, the place of the hyper real. Imitating the appearance of the historic city, they systematically remove all its defects, being safe, free of traffic and clean. They are easy to reach by car, there's parking space and all the complementary facilities to the shops are provided[9]:

> «It's a cross between Disneyland and a medieval village. A small town. Fake, naturally. Fake windows, fake balconies, even the walls themselves are fake. But it performs the functions of the village, surrogates it, replaces it […] You come, stroll around, window shop. Some people buy. A village with its square, palm trees, lamp posts, everything. Houses where nobody lives […] It is not a ghost town, but built as if there actually were inhabitants, so that the visitors can recognise it as their own, and instead of feeling like customers feel at home»[10].

The decline of one model, and, at the same time, the change in socio-economic conditions which that model had generated, constitute on of the starting points for the indentification of the *Pointers* and *Hypotheses* of the final chapter.

---

[8] The *factory outlet centres* take up in Western Europe two millions of square meters, twenty times the area of Paris. Just in Italy 322.000 square meters, second in ranking after Great Britain in «Largo Consumo», June 2009, p.7.

[9] The Designer Outlet Village in Serravalle Scrivia opened the 7th September 2000 and has been visited in the first ten months by 2.000.000 people (from the website of the enterprise, www.mcarthurglen.com).

[10] Cazzullo, A., *Outlet Italia*, Mondadori, Milano 2007, p. 8.

practice of consumption and spaces for goods

>>Gateway Theatre of Shopping, Durban

In contemporary shopping centres entertainment and leisure have more and more space in a continuous research of originality.

two examples of re-functionalization of commercial structures:

>>Royal Exchange, refurbishment in 1991 by Fitzroy Robinson Partnership and Peter Cook

>>Royal Exchange by Sir William Tite

The first Royal Exchange was designed by Thomas Gresham in 1571, the second, re-built after the fire in 1666, was designed by Edward Jarman in 1667-71. In 1838 the Royal Exchange has been again destroyed by fire and the new building, survived till today is designed by Sir William Tite.
In 1991 the project of the refurbishment has been committed to Fitzroy Robinson Partnership in collaboration with Peter Cook.

>>Chelsea Market, New York, Jeff Vandeberg

The Nabisco was an old biscuit factory with a complex built in between 1890 and 1940 on the 10th avenue in Manhattan; after closing was purchased by an investor that briefed the architect to re-use it without demolishing the existing buildings. The process rolled out for four years and transformed the spaces in a shopping centre themed on specialty food.

a department store, new intervention:

>>HEMA, Amsterdam, Merkx + Girod Architects, 1995

HEMA (an acronym for Hollandse Eenheidsprijzen Maatschappij Amsterdam, Dutch Standard Prices Company Amsterdam) it's a dutch chain department store. The chain is characterized by goods with a good quality and price, designed and produced by the brand itself. The design brief had to be applied to the 265 stores. The refurbishment project by Merkx+Girod, that involved also the communication design, works on efficient organisational and communication elements, remaining devoted to simplicity and pragmatism.

1.2.2.1

ONE STOP SHOP

«Ask not what you can do for your country. Ask what's for lunch».

Orson Welles

A new retail economy based on the mass-production of products and the containment of prices, produces new consumer goods which advertising promotes as essentials. This sparks the rise of the so called consumer society and marks the beginning of a cultural and commercial revolution which has not only altered the timing and rhythm of our daily routine, but has extended and standardised the market of convenience goods.

It is a retail business with deep roots in the financial sector, spurred on by the introduction of cashless forms of payment based on trust in the customer whereby the shopkeeper granted him credit in order to persuade him to consume more[1].

There was also a change in lifestyle and the average consumer no longer had the time to do their shopping in small speciality shops. This led to the rise of the *drugstore* and *supermarket*.

The supermarket, the origin of which Pevsner traces back to 1930 with the King Kullen in New York[2], deserves some consideration in it own right. Its architectural planning would seem to represent the destruction of any linguistic syntax: the greatest amount possible of free space and surfaces needs to be available in order to organise products, individual elements which are iconic in nature.

---

[1] In 1946 the Flatbush National Bank of New York starts a paying format without cash, a credit form very similar to our credit cards.

[2] Pevsner, N., *A History of Building Types*, Princeton Architectural Press, New York 1976, trad. it. *Storia e caratteri degli edifici*, Fratelli Palombi Editori, Roma 1986, p. 317.

>>A Safeway advertisement dated back in the '50

In Italy, il Carosello[3] was a television programme that changed the way of communicating which provided the impetus for the consequent change even in the place where shopping is done. The mainly female public approached the new distribution system with prudence and awe, this system which required the mechanism of self-service, or doing their shopping often without any mediation or mediators.

> «There was much talk of supermarkets in Italy in June 1956 when, on the occasion of an international congress on food distribution, the United States Department of Agriculture, in collaboration with the National Association of Food Chains, set up a display supermarket at Eur in Rome, a supermarket over one thousand square metres in area [...]. In the thirteen days it was there, it was visited by over 450,000 people, more than nineteen groups of specialist operators [...] and whipped up a frenzy of interest in the mass media»[4].

In 1956, the Standa chain in Naples opened a food market within the department store, whereas the first large food supermarket was opened in Milan in 1957, on the premises of the disused factory in Viale Regina Giovanna, later to become part of the Esselunga chain.

For Italian society, with the tragedy of the Second World War barely a decade in the past, the supermarket was one of the symbols of modernity, and along with the television and the automobile (the legendary Fiat 500), became an symbol of the economic boom.

The new supermarkets no longer had weighing scales. The goods

---

[3] *Carosello* is a name of a television programme on channel Programma Nazionale della RAI gone on the air from 1957 to the 1st of January 1977; it was a mix of comics and advertisements suggestions.

[4] Scarpellini, E., *La spesa è uguale per tutti*, Marsilio, Venezia 2007, p. 41.

practice of consumption and spaces for goods

came pre-packaged and ready to go, already weighed by the producer and distributors. Retail was starting to be organised like an industrial business, more like a factory than the old-style family-run shop, and even the external appearance changed as the window display gave way to the new advertisements.

In 1957, when Fiat introduced the five day working week leaving the workers free for two whole days, this brought about yet another change in social habits and brought the menfolk into contact with the new *commercial lifestyle*.

>>Best, Venturi-Scott Brown, facade decoration

three examples that subvert the design rules for the interior of supermarkets:

>>Publix on the Bay, Miami Beach, Wood and Zapata, 2000
Publix, named after a cinema, is popular for good quality and low prices, usually sold in anonymous spaces.
The project of Miami starts from the problem of the parking that wasn't enough on the plot. The design transform that need putting the parking on the roof, creating am unusual supermarket building.

>>M-Preis, Rainer Köberl & Astrid Tschapelier, Wenns, 2001
«The Seriously Sexy Supermarket» it's the slogan of this austrian chain of supermarkets that introduced great innovation both on the outside then on the interior of the space.
Interiors are very simple, with floor and walls painted black to let the goods stand out.
Against current idea that to concentrate on shopping is better not to have a view outside, they open up round windows looking at the Alps.

>>M-Preis Supermarket, Dominique Perrault Architecte, Wattens, 2003
The same chain of supermarkets propose a compete transparent facade looking at the landscape.

two projects that take inspiration from the rigid spatial organization of supermarkets:

>>Halfords Auto Depot, Swansea, UK, Ben Kelly Design, 1999

Halford at the end of the '90 started a re-branding to change typology of shop: from highstreet to superstore model.

Auto Depot deals with goods and services for cars and motorbikes.

The interior deign, very pragmatic, underline the client's journey in first place. The space layout is organized strictly with supermarket shelving and graphic very strongly refers to street traffic.

>>Hushush, Tokyo, Harry & Allen Associates, 2000

The main character of the shop is determined by materials and geometry.

The layout, that takes inspiration from the geometrical scheme of the supermarket, uses built-in furniture: one meter deep walls containing all the functions need; differentiation is done by use of materials: concrete for Basic department, mirror for Trendy one, clack for children's clothes, steel toiletry department and wood for the cash desk. Interruptions in the walls give visual communication in the store.

1.2.3

BILBAO EFFECT[1]

In 1997 the Bilbao Guggenheim, designed by Frank Gehry, was inaugurated. The *Bilbao effect* is the process that has transformed, through the construction of a landmark, a city of little interest into a mecca with thousands of visitors a day; this new synergy that sees the collaboration of brands and celebrated designers, promoted and facilitated by the planning instruments of the city, has been so successful as to literally transform the city centres of the biggest cities in the world in recent years.

Up until the mid 90's, places of commerce had never played such an important cultural role.

Architects worked on museums, public buildings and skyscrapers and the world of commerce was always relegated to a secondary position, even though there are cases of excellence which saw the stars of the architectural scene dealing with these themes.

The opposite is also true, insofar as brands never thought of linking their names to the aesthetics, promoted by the name of a specific architect, or by another brand.

This new partnership that sees the big names in the world of fashion working alongside the big names in the world of architecture makes one think about how the cultural climate has changed.

The start of this process can be traced back to 1996 when Calvin Klein asked John Pawson to design his flagship shop on Madison Avenue, New York: the ethereal shop, completely white, in complete contrast to the others, is similar to an art gallery where the fashion items can take on a

---

[1] Paraphrasing «*Beaubourg effect*» in Baudrillard, J., *Simulacri e impostura. Bestie, Beaubourg, apparenze e altri oggetti*, Cappelli, Bologna 1980, p. 24; Baudrillard maintains that the transformation in show of the building Beaubourg correspond to a lack of content for a commercial purpose; Beaubourg means for the first time for culture, what ipermarket means for goods.

new value and legitimise themselves; along with the image of the space for commerce, changes the way of displaying the goods which become rarefied translating the value of the goods themselves to the atmosphere one breathes. The shop had enormous success and was able to grow exponentially the value of the Calvin Klein brand name; the same route, the same language was subsequently copied in other experiences, such as Michael Gabellini for Jill Sander or Richard Gluckman for Helmut Lang. Recently, and especially in the last ten years, we are witnessing considerable experimentation in which places of commerce are playing a leading role, with different scales and types of intervention.

The *retailscape* in the 21st century is dotted with innovative elements on the whole range of types of places of commerce: it introduced new phenomena and developed new synergies between different consumer sectors, as in the case of co-branding, by experimenting and reinterpreting practices and places of commerce from days gone by.

The flagship store phenomenon, extensively covered by recent literature, has been consolidated by carrying out single operations entrusted to a joint venture between companies (mostly belonging to the luxury segment of the market) and individual professionals; minimalism has remained a stylistic key while marketing strategy has gradually become more refined. Important brands propose innovative formats which use the connotations of the container (Inside and out) and the organization of the products displayed with the primary objective of reinforcing brand awareness in the market. The instruments used are, apart from the brilliance of the individual designers, *visual merchandising* communication: «marketing projects that use architecture to change the city», as Giandomenico Amendola maintains[2] .

However, the flagship store model is not the only successful one; co-branding, the strategic display of different brands, even with goods belonging to completely different consumer areas, gives rise to new

---

[2] Amendola, G., "Luoghi, nonluoghi e superluoghi del commercio" in A.A.V.V., *La civiltà dei superluoghi*, Damiani editore, Bologna 2007.

practice of consumption and spaces for goods

types of retail spaces which see many different brands being put side by side under the same roof (multilogo) rather than the functional contamination with environments not strictly linked to the sale of the goods in question: plants and gift and fancy goods, bookshops with cafés and restaurants.

«The architecture of shops feeds on the blood of every available thing: art and technology, ideas and culture; and it does it in order not to produce anything lasting, but to create a constant state of flux. At the moment in which it is finished the work is already destined to die»[3].

This brief overview of the contemporary scene highlights that it is a hub linked to the planning of retail spaces, involves ever more requirements and necessities from the world of production, communication and society. The traditional types are so profoundly transformed as to give rise to a reflection, developed in the last chapter *Pointers and Hypothesis*, on its state of change which makes it increasingly unrecognizable, at least if it is analysed through the filters of the abacus of its disciplinary components.

---

[3] Kaal, R., "The great equalizer", *Frame*, n. 38, May-June 2004, pp. 56-57.

7| Guggenheim Museum, Bilbao, 2010 (picture© Ardfern)

1.3

from the project of public happiness to the one of private shopping

«At the end of '800 (in the United States) the main features of that culture were the acquisition and the consumption as means to reach happiness; the cult of novelties; the democratization of wishes; and the value of money as a determining factor of the value of society»[1].

After 1850, between the first and the second industrial revolution[2], the general stores start to appear in the great cities[3]. Both from the point of view of the impact of the new trade structures on the city and of the appearance of this new genre as well as from the social point of view, this is an epochal revolution, capable of transforming deeply the

---

[1] Leach, W., *Land of desire: Merchants, Power and the Rise of New American Culture*, Pantheon Books, New York 1993, p.3.

[2] The first Industrial Revolution refers to the textile and metallurgical sectors in between 1780 and 1830; the second refers to the introduction of electricity, chemical products and petrol from 1870.

[3] In 1838 opens in Paris the Bon Marchè of Aristide Boucilant.

structure of social life till nowadays.

With the General Store, leisure is led to the dimension of consumption: this is where «consumers start to feel as a mass»[4].

> «Happiness is normally bound to relative consumption: it depends on how much our consumption is different from the one of our equals»[5].

The Declaration of Independence of United States of America of 1776 states that governments are created among people to protect their Inalienable Rights, i.e. Life, Freedom and seek for Happiness: a collective project, the pursuing of a common goal, involving everyone and keeping united a society which recognizes in the seek for its happiness an inalienable right for each component.

The role played by goods has been critic in the transformation of the concept and the perceiving of happiness: as the production capacity grew, the consumption capacity proportionally grew as well and happiness converted from an object to be pursued according a political collective project into a kind of individual gratification to be consumed even in a few minutes, just like any product.

At the beginning of '80 years, Margareth Tatcher stated that «society doesn't exist» thus definitively giving way to the idea that all political and social axioms have to be traced to the economical sphere of liberism.

> «The market brought down the wall, not economics»[6].

Trade turns into an organizing means beating our daily time and organizing our cities. From the New York Times' columns in 1979, Ada Louise Huxtable already pointed out that «selling cities like soaps»[7],

---

[4] Benjamin,W., *Das Passagen-Werk*, Suhrkamp, Frankfurt a. M. 1982, trad. it., *Paris, capitale del XIX secolo. I passages di Paris*, Einaudi, Torino 1986, p. 87.

[5] Bruni, L., Pelligra, V., a cura di, *Economia come impegno civile*, Città Nuova, Roma 2002, p. 113.

[6] Paolini, Marco, *I Miserabili, io e Margareth Tatcher*, play broadcasted by channel La7 for the commemoration of the twenty years from the demolition of Berlin Wall.

[7] Ada Louise Huxtable: «Selling cities like soaps», *New York Times*, 16th November 1979.

anticipating by more than a decade Christine Boyer's remarks in the famous text by Sorkin, according to which «civic tableau that have been redeveloped into socially upgraded, historicized, commercialized and privatized enclaves»[8].

In this epochal transformation it is no more the city which hosts the commercial network, but the commercial network hosts the city. Just as in the post-war years the production plants were a precise part of the city, divided into functional areas, nowadays there is a re-functionalization and the construction of buildings aimed to commercial use.

The extraordinary conceptual and physical power of machinery, its unlimited capacity to solve problems and optimise processes in a continuous development aimed to a mechanicistic view of the universe, has influenced the whole western thought and, last but not least, the way to organize the environment built.

During the last century, the culture of project, having its apex in the theorems of the Modern Movement, has focussed on the idea of centrality of industrial processes, capable of spreading on the market, inside society and in the organization of the inhabited environment, the refreshing power of the logics of the machine. In this view, setting as the core of the industrial process the logic of works, the commercial network, as well as communications or promotion, seemed to represent peripherical phenomena, which were necessary but collateral to the production and to the processes of industrial construction.

>>Three Minutes Happiness, Tokyo; the client's journey lasts for three minutes, of happiness.

Nowadays, production turns to be a collateral and far reality and doesn't

---

[8] Boyer, C., "Cities for sale: merchandising history at South Street seaport" in Sorkin, M., *Variation on a theme park: The New American City and the End of Public Space*, Hill and Wang, New York 1992.

represent any more the identity of the undertaking which replaced the control of the building processes with the direct management of the commercial strategies, representing as a whole the brand on the market and in the society. The system of the outlets, retail, commercial stores plays a key-role within the globalization process, being the sole interface between the market and the production system more and more spread and less recognizable.

«What characterizes today's western societies, as a matter of fact, is not the production of goods and nevertheless of the producers necessary for their creation. It is the consumers' production»[9].

The process already defined by Marx as *mercification of society* pervades all spaces, not only multiplying the types and the number of places where you can buy goods, but occupying places foreign to the trade of goods as function (hotels, restaurants, cinemas, museums, sport, health...) determining what Jeremy Rifkin defines as *cultural capitalism*[10].

«Roads, motorization, etc. have closely linked the periphery to the center, abolishing every material distance. Through television, the Center has enclosed the whole Nation, which was so historically differentiated and rich of original cultures. It has started a work of homologation destroying every authenticity and contradictions. It has imposed as a matter of fact its models. Which are the models wanted by the new industrialization, no more being satisfied with "a person consuming", but letting no more be conceivable ad ideology other than consumption. An neo-lay hedonism, blindly forgetting every humanistic value and blindly apart from human sciences»[11].

---

[9] Codeluppi, Vanni, *Il potere del consumo*, Bollati Boringhieri, Torino 2003, p. 8.

[10] Rifkin, Jeremy, *L'era dell'accesso. La rivoluzione della New Economy*, Mondadori, Milano 2000.

[11] Pasolini, P. P., "Sfida ai dirigenti della televisione", *Il Corriere della Sera*, 9 settembre 1973.

8| Barberino outlet (picture©Sailko)

1.3.1

FROM CONSUMPTION TO COMFORT, FROM *SHOPPING FOR* **TO** *SHOPPING AROUND*

«The aim of the play of consumption is not the desire either to acquire and possess or to amass a large fortune in the material, tangible sense, on the other hand it is the excitement for new sensations, never experienced before. Consumers are first of all gatherers of sensations: they are collectors of things only in a secondary and derived sense»[1]

Mankind has established a different link with the place of sale: from place of buying it turned into place of experience, knowledge and entertainment. The fulcrum turns therefore to be the personal experience of the individual: his own daily world, which is unique, the social context, characterized by personal relationships, between oneself and oneself and between oneself and others, the system of signs and meanings and tales, which are fundamental and characterizing the necessary differences to be respected as such.

The consumer's society produces first of all desires which are carried by communication. The purchase doesn't satisfy functional needs any more and turns to be the carrier of messages and feelings.

If planning was focussed on goods, governed by technology (escalator, air conditioning), now the main attention is driven to the consumer: the means of project had to address to other disciplines as consumers are no more considered as buyers of products but as persons with desires, feelings and different personalities.

The economics of experience derives from the necessity of companies of distinguishing themselves and from the realization that this is no longer possible trough the product.

---

[1] Bauman, Z., *Dentro la globalizzazione. Le conseguenze sulle persone*, Laterza, Roma-Bari 2001, p. 93.

Shopping definitively loses its functional feature and acquires more and more a role as entertainer: *just looking* has become a good reason to enter a shop, where often you just can have a look, get infos, spend some time, not necessarily to purchase.

The consumption of the product must be induced by something other than the product itself, which is no more capable of expressing subjectivity. It is necessary that the place of sale is also a place of entertainment, giving way to many contaminations with culture, sport as well as leisure.

>>Guinness Storehouse, Dublin

>>Federation Square, Lab architecture studio, Melbourne, 2004

a big car company organized a huge theme park with production and a big leisure park open to the public:

>>VW Autosstadt, Wolfsburg, Germany

Wolfsburg is the place chosen back in 1936 for the construction of the car factory, today one of the biggest of the world with brand as Audi, Seat, Škoda Auto, Bentley, Lamborghini and Bugatti. The Volkswagen group, design Autostadt, the first themo park on cars that is so far far so big. A perfect example of entertainment. visitors can walk from one pavilion to another, go to the museum go shopping and sleep at Ritz-Carlton.

1.4

«Architecture for Sale(s)»

«People enjoy the experience of buying, sometimes more than having the products themselves, because the moment of buying is one of enthusiastic fantasy and escape»[1].

Often the first impact of a city is influenced by the quality of its shops; shopwindows and signs tell the story of places and culture of the places where they are. According to Rem Koolhaas, *retail* is the greatest influencing power in modelling the modern city and just *retail* defines its quality. Downtown is again the heart of the matter after decades of abandon, emigration towards the suburbs and peripheries scattered with commercial centres.

However, it is its role which is changing, from historical centre, carrier of values, memory and traditions, to a privileged place, hosting the most

---

[1] Kelley, K. E., "Architecture for Sale(s)" in *Harvard Design Magazine*, n. 17, Fall 200/Winter 2003. The paper written by Kelley is an apologia against hypocrisy of who accuse retail to be immoral. According to the author, instead retail is «big opportunity for architects».

prestigious commercial sites.

In 1979, Mrs. Huxtable, in the a.m. report, from New York Times' columns, complained about the city selling its internal places «like soaps»[2].

City and territory are reduced to the role of spectators, rather than actors, in the re-definition of functions, of life relationships as well as of landscape.

> «[…] a landscape of the "city as order" to the "city as offer", as a possibility for the realization of the individual […]. The city doesn't draw any longer a social order […] materializing itself through an organization of space, with its avenues, public squares and monuments. It represents a system of offers of professional activities and employment […], services and products, relationships, sense, possible behaviours and, more specifically, milieus, tales, events, mobility structures[3]»

The City is no more an assembly of «architectural boxes» to become a territory of «commodity economics, exchange, information and service»[4].

The architectural system doesn't manage any longer to create environmental qualities to be perceived and shared. The quality of the retail network is nowadays one of the essential elements of the aesthetic and cultural quality of the city. Once upon a time the City hosted the commercial network, now the commercial network hosts the City.

>>Omotesando fashion district, Tokyo

To corroborate this thesis, from the point of view of the creation of extra-

---

[2] Huxtable, A. L., "Selling cities like soaps", *New York Times*, 16 January 1979.

[3] Bourdin, A., *La métropole des individus*, Éditions de l'Aube, La Tour d'Aigues 2005.

[4] Branzi, A., "Retailing in the globalization era", in AA.VV., *Places & Themes of Interiors Contemporary Research Worldwide*, Franco Angeli, Milano 2008.

practice of consumption and spaces for goods

urban commercial structures, the main character is once again the shape, the appearance of the historical city: on the one hand, protected and efficient artificial historical walls, on the other hand whole city areas, where the visit to monuments was replaced by the one to great fashion shops. A radicalization of the processes started with the appearance of commercial centres where a multitude of people, belonging to every walk in life, practically excluded from the historical city, reproduce the ideal of urban life in an artful context, whereby it derives a scenario of public pacified site.

This process has gone so far that it gives way to a role inversion: it becomes a new model of city in which not only people buy, but they live and work in a modern market-village reminding the factory-village, where there were housing opportunities but also plenty of public and social assistance services.

In the meanwhile, downtown, the flagship store, such as a show, becomes an ideal place for an exclusive demonstration of brands aimed to identify them with lifestyles and values as well. The commercial site turns into a place beyond architecture, in the dimension of the global market, where the system of the more complex industrial production combines technologically functional performance aspects with products and product families, such as communication and distribution, which thus became new essential components of a global enterprise. The complex system referred to extends the field of planning closely bound to industrial production, integrating it into new strategies from logics of the economical market evolving: goods, products, distribution and at last commercialization build up a whole context of economics of this new production system associated to communication and marketing.

>>West Edmonton Mall, Canada

11| Courtyard of a Shophouse in Malacca, Malaysia. (picture©Someformofhuman)

1.4.1

POST-PRODUCTION

For a long time efforts have been made to not contaminate the *historic* city with functions and activities of a commercial nature so as not to be subordinate to the market. This policy has in fact delegated private individuals to work according to their own interests, thereby distorting not only the spirit of the places but also the role of planning.

The idea that concentration of businesses being set against historical and culturally consolidated area has been replaced by the hypothesis that reconfirm the role of revitalizer of heritage locations on the retail space[1].

Reconsidering the social and urban value that these places can have, acting as a stimulus for the infrastructure connected to them, commerce forges new relationships with the machinery and forms of the historical fabric.

We will no longer speak about commercialisation of space in a speculative sense, but of redesigning for commercial use which will reintroduce the historical role of engine of the city's economy and an element of control on globalized management. Commerce once again starts working on the city, carrying out an urgent task with a noble objective, stripping itself of its meaning insofar as it refers solely to consumerism[2].

Andrea Branzi commented recently that «a new form of architecture is evolving out of the study and role of interior design and a new relationship between project and urban context»[3].

The discipline of interiors has the instruments to operate on the renewal and reuse of the existing patrimony, to claim the necessity for the new by grafting the new

---

[1] «Locations: transport interchanges, heritage locations, web» in Dawson, J., *The Future of Retailing*, Symposium, Edinburgh, 21 February 2002.

[2] «In the next 20 years retail will be all about values», *The future of retailing*, Nyenrode European Business Forum, Report Retail Forum, Nyenrode Business Universiteit.

[3] Branzi, A., speech at the Seconda Conferenza Nazionale sull' Architettura e il design d'interni "Interiors In The Re-Use Of Exhisting Buildings. Tradition And Research", Iuav, Venezia, 24-25 October 2007.

onto the old, adding to the original space that of its transformation, making it an interpreter of some of the everyday emergencies.

>>Clarke Quay, Will Allsop, Singapore

>>The Jen Library, Savannah College of Art and Design, Savannah

different scale of project; the urban scale for:

>>Fünf Höfe, Munich, Herzog & de Meuron, 2003
An urban scale project that includes offices, apartments, shops, exhibition spaces, restaurants and a bank. The entire lot is 23.888 square meters. Fünf Höfe (literally Five Courtyards) is an articulated path that connects the five yards.

the building scale for:

>>The Boekhandel Selexyz Dominicanen, Maastricht, Merkx and Girod Architects, WWW
The library, that has been appointed like the most beautiful of the world, it's been set into a former church. Perception of the interior space and of proportion is preserved with the insertion of independent volumes, without any structural modifications.

and the one of the single unit:

>>Maison Martin Margiela

The collection of Martin Margiela is conceptually and practically constructed with old clothes pieces reinvented in new products. The shops are designed in the same way; the one in London is in a building that has been re-functionalized many times: from stable to artist's workshop and art gallery. Walls are left as found and furniture is mainly second-hand. Has said from one of the employee «it's the way of Maison Margiela to erase the shop» (da: Bingham, N., *The New Boutique. Fashion and Design*, Merrel, London 2005, trad. it. *Le nuove boutique*, Idea Books, Milano 2005, p.35), an approach that works on memory.
The shop in Paris is a former industrial design school, a former fast food the one in Taiwan, and an office building the one in Milano.

12| Magna Plaza, Amsterdam, 1992

The building was built in between 1895 and 1899 and was the Head Post Office. The design is by Cornelis Peters alumnus of Cuypers, author of the Central Station and the Rijkmuseum. In 1992, city administration added this building to the list of heritage historical buildings and advertised a competition for its re-functionalization. Magna Plaza is the bigger shopping centre in the city and from an interior point of view is interesting how conservation and brand image issues have been work out.

1.5

buying
ideas

practice of consumption and spaces for goods

In 1960 the boutique appears again in a highly developed consumption economy and turns to be expression of a newly emerged individualism, non-conformist design and new ideas about lifestyle, deriving from the youth protests of those years.

The customers of these shops are consumers of those ideas and the places follow the motto «creativity to the power».

The sense of freedom of the new generation certainly also entailed consuming more.

Some of these shops marked deeply the culture of those years: forerunners of a radical change in the retail world, they understood first that the most precious thing to sell was not the kind of commodity but an idea, a concept.

Shops like Sex and World's End, by Vivienne Westwood and Malcolm McLaren at King's Road in London were forerunners of the successive *concept stores*.

Among these, central was the Biba case, by which Elio Fiorucci was inspired –he says- for the innovative shops in Milan and New York. Biba has totally revolutionized the concept itself of point of sail. The first shop, opened in 1964 by Barbara Hulanicki and his husband Steven Fitz-Simon at an old chemist's was so successful among the public that in 1968 they started mail-order shopping for their products.

The huge success let Biba move every two years to open a new shop with the ambition to create a Biba *lifestyle environment*. The dream came true when in 1973 they bought the old Derry and Toms building at Kensington High Street: an emporium inspired by the general stores of the 20's but with a more relaxed mood, thinking that the retail needed a democratization. At the beginning of 70's Biba was the first general store to open in London after the Second World War and in 1974, it became the greatest touristic attraction after Tower of London.

>>The Beatles, Apple Boutique, London, 1967; The Beatles sold clothes, housewares, foreseeing marketing operations that will invade the market in the '80.

Big Biba invented the lifestyle concept: they sell under they brand a great variety of goods from dresses by the stylist Hulanicki to cosmetics, fancy goods, and even food. It was a beautiful *fantasy palace* giving to the retail the indulgence of the lifestyle of those years.

practice of consumption and spaces for goods

two among the most influent shops on future concepts:

>>Bazaar, King's Road, London, 1955
The first Bazaar opened in King's Road in 1955. After a few years the second one opened in 1957, in Brompton Road designed by Terence Conran: steel, plexiglas and glassfiber for the first time were used in an interior.

>>Big Biba, London, 1974
The new shop has a new interior concept inspired to the Glam Rock; Biba become stage for trends, looking like a film set where Art Deco was meeting the Victorian Style. At Biba's played The New York Dolls, i Liberace, the Manhattan Transfer and Brian Ferry filmed here the video fort the song "Let's Stick Together". Biba closes down in 1975, due to the crisis and today is replaced by a Marks & Spencer branch.

a contemporary concept store that has translated, with a lot of investment, what in the '60 was already a statement:

>>NikeTown, New York, LeClere Architects, 1998
Niketown is a concept store, a mix in between a shop and a themed park; «I wanted a living building, something that showed the way for the future and in which architecture come to life. We were fighting to capture people's "mind space"» says John Hoke, image creative director (from Cliff, S., *50 Trade Secrets of Great Design Retail Spaces*, Rockport Publishers, Gloucester U.S.A. 1999).
The shop is a city itself and you need to get a passport to get in.

1.6

unisex
shopper

practice of consumption and spaces for goods

Around the 1980's, many housewives in the United States, even in the suburban areas, began to work outside the home. Today, two thirds of American women have a job and from a commercial viewpoint, this profound change in the social structure has created entire new sectors in the industry, changing both the times and the manner in which shopping is done. Work commitments added to the time required for getting to and from the workplace, considerably reduce the time available for buying and cooking food. In order to respond to the new requirements and the new availability of time and money, the food industry and restaurant sector came up with new products combined with services. This was the origin of prepackaged precooked foods, frozen foods and take-aways. Changing the role as consumer of women, not only were new environments created to host the new products, but there was also a change in the prerequisites according to which these spaces were designed. The woman was no longer the sole figure delegated by the family to manage the household and therefore also the shopping, but possessed an economic independence which was seen by the producers as a resource. The woman was no longer the sole interlocutor in the commercial sector and the structure of the retail outlet adapted to these new consumer typologies which included a wide range of gender and age categories.

But now women also became new customers for certain types of goods which, until then, had been the sole prerogative of men. It is very interesting, for example, to see how the interior layout of jeweller's changed. What had been a type of shop traditionally visited by men coming in to buy a gift for their wives, daughters, or girlfriends, became, like all other shops, another place for anyone to come in even just to buy a present for themselves. When men were the typical customer, the interior was laid out with counters where the sales assistant displayed the jewellery so that it could be seen and examined. If the customer was a woman, there needed to be space to try on the jewellery, and the customer needed to be able to look at her reflection. This meant changes to the lighting, furnishings and layout of the interior.

These factors led to the creation of sales outlets which we could call unisex, where the identification of the type of customer is no longer based mainly on age, gender, or even purchasing power, but rather cultural affinity which binds groups of people with certain consumer habits.

>>Rosie the Riveter, is a song's title of the '40. Rosie became the symbol of the new working women.

13| Breakfast at Tiffany's, Blake Edwards, 1961

1.7

free
entrance

practice of consumption and spaces for goods

The arrival on the scene of self service was another element that revolutionised the hierarchy and roles of the internal spaces of places of commerce, knocking down the barriers between customer and seller. It emerged after the Second World War and it was closely linked to the development of other industries such as packaging and it allowed for the expansion of display areas for consumer goods. Furthermore it optimized the number of sales staff.

In the beginning the customers, used to dealing with their trusted sales assistant who mediated for them in making their purchases, were so perplexed by this new system that the shops, in some cases, had to even hire actors to demonstrate how easy it was to shop in this new way.

To benefit from the self service system, which saved both time and money, the customers had to learn new skills, be informed, aware of the differences in price and quality, so that they could make decisions on their own. For their part the companies had to find new ways of communicating since now the customers had to choose for themselves.

The role of the shop assistant changed dramatically now that the customer was free to touch the goods (even more so in the case of high-priced goods), and they stood close to them, giving them advice as if they were a close friend. This was so different to what happened, for example, in the Knize shop of Adolf Loos, where the sales counter and the sales clerk behind it clearly defined the roles and the ways in which the commercial transaction was carried out.

From a disciplinary point of view, the impact of such a change influenced both the study of the movement of customers (who were allowed to go around freely without being obstructed) and the equipment for display areas which had to make the goods accessible and organised according to a certain logic.

It was at this precise moment that graphic communication, signs, entered into the space, to orient the customer in their choice of specific goods or to draw their attention to events of particular relevance.

1.7.1

«L'EMPIRE DES SIGNES»[1]

> «Shop space today is no more than an extension of television, newspapers and magazine advertising. They provide the space where consumer fantasies can come true»[2].

In consumer society which shifts the value of the inherent qualities of the product into its communicative value, consumption comes to be bound to the immaterial qualities of the latter. These are the qualities which have the role of embodying sense and therefore, of being capable of communicating with a range of expressive strategies.

Since the 1990's in particular, fashion communicates by means of images and signs, information which is difficult to synthesise in the product and is therefore transformed into signs, symbols, communication and space for goods.

The appearance of what has become known as the *silent salesman*[3], and the consequent disappearance of the owner-shopkeeper brought about a radical transformation in the layout of spaces. Communication went global and no longer only concerned advertisements and signs in the shop windows.

Sophisticated marketing tools like *advertising* and *merchandising* were introduced, and changes made to the product itself with *packaging* and the introduction of price tags. Changes were made to shop decor, furnishings, moving in the direction of a type of organisation which reduced the number of staff. Everything had to communicate the value

---

[1] Barthes, R., *L'empire des signes*, Skira, Genève 1970, trad. it. *L'impero dei segni*, Einaudi, Torino, 1984, 1992.

[2] Gottdiener, M., *The Theming of America*, Westview Press, Boulder 1997, p. 90.

[3] Il termine è stato coniato dal designer James Pilditch nel 1961 riferendosi al packaging; Pilditch, J., *The Silent Salesman: How to Develop Packaging That Sells*, Business Books Ltd., London 1973 (da Vernet, D., de Wit, L., Boutiques and other Retail Spaces, Routledge, New York 2007).

of the meaning of the brand.

Over the past thirty years, the retail sector has worked on the form of identification of the brand. The history of the evolution of advertising could be written side by side with that of architecture and retail space[4]. Roughly speaking, this evolution can be traced back to three main phases: the semiotic phase, the post-semiotic phase, and the phenomenological phase.

>>Calvin Klein, John Pawson, Madison Avenue, New York, 1995

Semiotics operates through the transfer of values by means of a process of association. A famous example is the shop which John Pawson built in New York for Calvin Klein in 1995: the architectural backdrop plays the role of primary sign; the minimal, rich style and the expensive materials communicate a sense of refinement which is transferred from the surroundings the designer's clothes.

During the 1980's, studies were published by the eminent scholars of advertising theory Robert Goldman and John Papson on Generation X[5]: the authors described this public as «sophisticated readers of semiotic messages, cynical and bored by what they saw»[6]. The post-semiotic phase, whose main proponents were Jacques Derrida, Umberto Eco and Diesel' advertising campaign.

Roland Barthes, introduced the concept of intertextuality: a language

---

[4] Cairns, G., "From semiotics to phenomenology in advertising and retail design" in AA.VV., *Places & Themes of Interiors Contemporary Research Worldwide*, Franco Angeli, Milano 2008.

[5] Generation X concerns people born in between 1965 and 1981 and is the tile of a book by Charles Hamblett and Jane Deverson. The work, commissioned by the review «Woman's Own», was concerning interviews to teenagers; the interviews underlined a generation promiscuous and anti-establishment and unfit to be published on the review.

[6] Goldman, R., Papson, S., *Sign Wars*, Guildford Press, London. 1996.

which allows for an unstable interpretation of signs through the use of multiple and contradictory references within the same text.

In the Happy Valley advertising campaign produced by Diesel in the 90's, the semiotic structure of the happy young protagonists becomes a parody of itself in a surreal context; the artificialness is underlined by the slogan «happiness, dreams, pleasure and even freedom are all sponsored by Diesel».

Rei Kawakubo too, with Comme des Garçons, uses architecture in a similar manner, especially in the Guerilla Stores and the design of Dover Street Market in London. In Dover Street Market, artists and designers created installations which refer back to the archetype of the market, with an anti-glamour underground patina; an ironic parody of luxury and beauty to condemn the way in which retail spaces had become so standardised.

The phenomenological approach explored new codes in order to attract attention, using forms of hidden advertising and hybrid retail: there is no longer any attempt to attract public attention to the advertising.

Vexed Generation has a strong sociopolitical programme and, in its displays, like the White Shop, transfers values which have no direct connection with the goods: an installation which talks about civil rights, urban pollution and safety. The shop window is painted white and the interior is always filmed on closed circuit cameras which transmit images to a screen outside.

>>Dover Street Market, Rei Kawakubo, London

1.7.2

«IT IS ABOUT EDITING THE WORLD FOR THEIR CUSTOMERS»[1]

«We are collectors or artistic directors…. Our objective is not commercial but cultural!»[2]

On the one hand consumers are more refined and demanding, on the other the great multitude of choice of goods of any type is leaving the consumers in the hands of those who are able to make a selection. A new idea of curators who preselect the goods to be sold, worn, read or eaten.

«All museums will become big stores and all big stores will become museums», Andy Warhol claimed. That which seems to be the new frontier of *curated consumption*, presents us with shops that resemble more and more museums and art galleries. There are ever more analogies that can be found in the use of the two disciplines which are contaminating each other, almost to the point of confusion.

>>MoMA, New York, every year the commercial area grows while the one dedicated to exhibition gets smaller

It's the shop, its name, its place to become the instrument able to represent the identity of the brand; the *space setting* is similar to a museum setting, engaging a cultural relationship within the shop and the client, aware of doing qualified shopping choices.

Among the most famous of these types that we can find are Colette in

---

[1] Johnston, L., Agneessens, S., "The Culture of Commerce", *GDR Creative Review*, n. 26, September 2007.

[2] Renny Ramakers on the role of Droog Design for the shop Mandarina Duck in Paris, in Tucker, J., *Retail desire: Design, Display and Visual Merchandising*, trad. it. *Punti vendita e visual merchandising*, Rotovision, Logos, Crans-prés-Céligny, Modena 2003, p. 7.

Paris, the Conran shop n London and Anthropologie in New York.

We have already spoken of Biba in *Buying ideas* and among the forerunners of this approach we cannot fail to mention the case of Fiorucci.

>>Fiorucci, 1967

In 1967 the Fiorucci shop opened in Milan, designed by the sculptress Amelia Dal Ponte inspired by Biba of London. The functional programme, besides the part dedicated to the real shop, included a *vintage* market part a restaurant and a space for theatrical shows.
Enzo Biagi, in his columns of the Corriere della Sera newspaper, defines Elio Fiorucci as «the man who has destroyed fashion»[3], underestimating perhaps the effect that this approach would have on the subsequent history of retail spaces. Fiorucci invented a new way of working, by experimenting with collaborating with the most innovative designers, graphic artists and photographers, among whom were Bruce Andrews, Oliviero Toscani, Roger Corona and Gianni Viviano and by proposing artistic, musical and culinary performances in his store. In 1979 Fiorucci opened a shop on 59th Street in New York, entrusting Ettore Sottsass, Andrea Branzi and Franco Mirabelli with the interior design. This shop was so successful that Andy Warhol chose it for the launch of his new magazine *Interview*. Marc Jacobs, in a recent interview declared «every time we try to do something new we seem to end up doing Fiorucci»[4].

---

[3] Biagi, E., "L'uomo che ha distrutto la moda", *Corriere della sera*, 1976.

[4] Marenco Mores, C., *Da Fiorucci ai Guerrilla Stores*, Marsilio, Venezia 2006, p.60.

three examples of *edited consumption:*

>>Colette, Paris, Arnaud Montigny, 1997

Colette, named after one of the partners, occupies a three storey building with a total surface of 250 square meters: at the ground floor there's a restaurant open 24 hours, at the first floor beauty products, design items, electronic accessories and trainers, and at the second floor men's and women's clothing; there is also a mezzanine for temporary exhibitions. «One of the most important ideas was to have an opening around the large central staircase so it's possible to see up and down to the other levels [...] We didn't want to make it a loft space. It had to have more presence» (Arnaud Montigny e Cyril Issaverdens from Cliff, S., *50 Trade Secrets of Great Design Retail Spaces*, Rockport Publishers, Gloucester U.S.A. 1999, p. 177). Regarding the interior's fittings, they had to be as flexible as possible in order to be moved or substitute.

>>The Conran Shop, CD Partnership, London, 1997

Terence Conran, architect and founder of Habitat, is the inventor of the concept of lifestyle applied to design furniture and housewares.

>>Anthropologie, Pompei AD, New York,1992

Every Anthropologie shop' design has a strong connection with the place and local culture. «There's a deliberated blurred line that goes from merchandise, to artefacts, to furniture, to fittings, to architecture» (from Cliff, S., *50 Trade Secrets of Great Design Retail Spaces*, Rockport Publishers, Gloucester U.S.A. 1999, p.141).

practice of consumption and spaces for goods

THIS SHOP ROCKS

1.8

«Guerrilla marketing»

Levinson wrote his book «Guerrilla Marketing»[1] in 1993.

According to Jeremy Rifkin, one time culture preceded the market, now markets determine culture.

For many years, the organization of the spaces of commerce has been rigorously dictated by surveys belonging to the marketing sector, which statistically found out that, in the commercial centres, we cannot purchase as soon as we enter and that we don't even remark anything within ten meters from the entrance. Today, even this simple rule is put in crisis by the change of customers' habits. Because of that, just at the entrance of supermarkets, there are some areas, the so called C-store (convenience store), shops with a limited sales area and with a strict product assortment in comparison with the common-use goods. Even Tiffany, the famous jeweller's of New York, has something similar at

---

[1] Levinson, J. C., *Guerrilla Marketing*, Houghton Mifflin, Boston 1993.

the entrance of the shop with an area dedicated to a selection of small, pre-packed jewels.

The change in customers' features, which is hardly classifiable within the limits of the old concept of *target*, put in crisis the dictates of what has always been considered nearly like a precise science.

In their book of 1999[2], Joe Pine and Jim Gilmore pointed out that *service economy* had turned out into *experience economy*: from a property culture to the one of experience. The experience culture as we have seen, has given impulse and life to new spaces for commerce, characterized by the contamination between commercial activities and activities bound to the entertainment and leisure sector.

In the same year, Berndt Schmitt[3] pointed out that experience is divided into five different modules, including sensory perception, affective reaction, as well as the cognitive, physical and collective experiences.

After nearly a decade, Albert Boswijk, Thomas Thijssen and Ed Peelen, with the book *The experience economy: a new perspective*[4], redefine the terms of the matter.

The experience economy described by Pine and Gilmore includes a passive perception determined by stimuli of economic nature. The next step is the active involvement of the consumer into the self-defined co-creation experience, implying a change in the creation of value determined by different economic models requiring more transparency and social responsibility.

> «Asking consumers about their purchase behaviour by using traditional questionnaires
> is hardly useful. As a matter of fact, the majority of advertising doesn't work: 9 out
> of 10 of the new brands launched on the market fail after 3 months [...] the sensorial

---

[2] Pine, J., Gilmore, *The Experience Economy*, Harvard Business School Press, Boston, 1999, trad. it. *L'economia delle esperienze: oltre il servizio*, Etas, Milano, 2000.

[3] Schmitt, B., *Experiential marketing*, Free Press, 1999. trad. it. *Marketing esperienziale: come sviluppare l'esperienza di consumo*, Franco Angeli, 2006.

[4] Boswijk, A., Thijssen, A., Peelen, E., *The experience economy, a new perspective*, Pearson Education, Upper Saddle River (NJ) 2007.

practice of consumption and spaces for goods

immersive areas will be the next step in the retail sales»[5].

In the revolutionary model, indicated by them with step 3.0, both parties, i.e. producers and consumers, are able to insert variables into the process. The new consumer is characterized by the different attitude towards rules, authority and the nation-state, organized through associationism types, better representing socio-cultural affinities. According to Paco Underhill, «the magic bullet of the XX century marketing is word-of-mouth»[6].

---

[5] Intervista a Martin Lindtsrom in "Sensorial marketing. Profuno di dollari", *D di Repubblica*, n. 648, 2008, p.48.

[6] Underhill, P., *The Call of the Mall: A Walking Tour Through the Crossroads of Our Shopping Culture*, Simon and Schuster, New York 2004, trad. it. *Antropologia dello shopping. Il fascino irresistibile dei centri commerciali*, Sperling & Kupfer, Torino 2004, p. 89.

1.8.1

«NO LOGO»[1]

> «Just as medieval society was balanced on God and the Devil, ours is balanced on consumerism and its denunciation»[2].

Freedom of choice in western capitalist societies always coincides with the freedom to buy; nobody questions the capitalist model but rather one tries to govern it using its own means, from within, in other words using commercial types of choices. Associationism[3] and the *no global* movement itself do not question capitalism but rebel against companies that operate in a non-ethical way towards consumers and workers.

Purchasing power has become our defining characteristic and our most effective weapon, this being the instrument with which battles for global rights are fought which aspire to finding justice in the consolation of the homogeneous nature of economics.

«The consumer is the non-professional counterpart of the business»[4], able to profoundly influence the structure of the company. Many companies, aware of the sensitivity of consumers with regard to certain themes, such as sustainability or protecting animals, have centred their image entirely around these themes.

The demands of the so called *no global* movement make a deep analysis of the mechanisms which govern the retail world, by highlighting how the loss of interpersonal relationships or of local points of reference are capable of causing these models to implode which, by distancing themselves ever more from the needs of the new consumers, lose all of their sense of value.

---

[1] Klein, N., *No logo*, Knopf Canada, Toronto 2000, trad. it. Baldini e Castoldi, Milano 2002.

[2] Baudrillard, Jean, *The Consumer Society*, Sage, London 1970, *La società dei consumi*, il Mulino, Bologna 1976.

[3] Consumers International (CI) is a non-governative association (ONG) that represents group of consumers worldwide, with 230 organizations in 113 countries. The goal is to promote a better society through the defence of consumer's rights.
It was born in 1960 as International Organisation of Consumers Unions (IOCU).

[4] Bessone, M., *Contratti del Mercato e teorie del consumo*, Padova, 1976, p. 621.

1.9

retail or virtual?

«By now, a contraction of the universe of the material objects would be started, objects to be replaced by processes and services becoming more and more immaterial [...]. Personally I'm not convinced about that [...]. As a matter of fact, it means going beyond the common sense, considering as plausible that, in the future, life of mankind [...] can take place within the limits of a thick web of mirages, from which nobody could escape»[1].

In 1985, the great exhibition *Les Immatériaux,* planned by the French philosopher Lyotard is held at The George Pompidou Centre in Paris. The appearance of the digital sector imposes a change of mind in the definition of matter: it's the end of Modern age.

Especially in the last decade, the World Wide Web revolution became such a widespread tool to bring the traditional commerce to collapse. With a huge increase of the volume of products purchased on Internet,

---

[1] Maldonado, T., *Reale e virtuale*, Feltrinelli, Milano 1992, pp. 10-12.

the traditional space had to start a process of change of mind about its meaning, especially towards the youngest customers using informatic tools in a natural way. A new challenge, able to introduce essential innovations going beyond the aesthetic aspect and wondering what is their role and the true expectations of the new public.

Web consumption is particularly successful in two conditions: either when the goods are very cheap or when they are well known, such as when you buy a book or a brand in which you already placed your trust. In 2000 Paddy Meehan, *oki-ni*'s inventor, got over the rule of selling on Internet greater quantities at a cheaper price. The challenge was to use the same means but sell small quantities at a higher price. At the beginning it had to be just an on-line business, but fearing the times were not mature yet, they created also a physical place where it was possible to see and touch the goods and place orders (oki-ni products are customized). Thus, the initial protection from the fear of realizing a too futuristic project, in reality turned out to be the winner hands down as, at he beginning, the 80% of orders was placed on line, but from the shop. The shop started to be a fashion place, there was the wireless technology and people went there to spend some time and work with their own laptop[2].

>>Prada Epicentre, OMA, New York; virtualily unto Into shop through display settings

---

[2] Interview by the author to Paddy Meehan, September 2008.

E-commerce, in spite of its countless benefits, brings to a failure of one of the essential features of shopping: the interpersonal relationship. Future shops have to find the right equilibrium to combine the coldness and the convenience of the virtual tool with the warmth of the material world.

the concept store that combines the potentiality of the virtual world with the materiality of the physical space:

>>Oki-ni, 6a Architects, Londra, 2001

«Rarity is an innocence proof» (from oki-ni website http://www.oki-ni.com). The clients buy online limited editions of famous brands.
Paddy Meehan, Oki-ni's inventor, considers the shop as a gallery: he didn't want a shop but an friendly place where pieces of clothing were mixed to books and magazines as in a museum bookstore. The space itself should have been transitory; the interior , completely made of russian oak, is like a shell set in the existing space.

2

spaces for goods

2.1

introduction

practice of consumption and spaces for goods

In his famous book which came out in 1996[1] Negroponte prophetized the imminent de-materialisation of material goods. On the other hand, in recent years there has been a massive focus in the design world on the creation of spaces for displaying these goods, to such an extent that design of commercial space has become a discipline in its own right and increasingly labelled *Retail Design*.

This section will first illustrate the links between the practice of consumption, the mechanisms which regulate it, and the main players in the field, before dealing with the disciplinary debate. *Retail Design* plays a fundamental role in the functioning of commercial intermediation, responding as it must to the needs of both demand and supply.

The design of retail space involves complex categories which are only

---

[1] Negroponte, N., *Being Digital*, First Vintage Books Editions, New York 1996, trad. it. *Essere digitali*, Sperling & Kupfer, Torino 1996.

partially directly linked to the production and distribution of goods. Analysis of the spaces within which consumers relate to goods is a key to studying society and an indicator of what dynamics govern these processes which influence customs, the shape of cities and communication media. As we have already seen above, from a formal viewpoint, space devoted to retail business lacks a real form of its own: its is multiform, organised into a variety of different types and has no true stylistic tradition. Over time, it has assumed shapes arising from the institution of relationships with its own surroundings, whether this is strongly defined or a *non places*, distinguished by its typological elasticity and gathering within itself types which are disparate from both a qualitative and quantitative viewpoint: retail spaces are the market, bazaar, individual shop, department store, mall, supermarket and also the virtual retail space that is the web. From the perspective of the role which retail spaces have played throughout the course of history, it is evident how it is always a place of relation and interaction par excellence, able to relate with other functions and play the role of interface and amalgam.

What makes the study of retail space today interesting (in the same way as what is happening in other fields of design such as exhibition design) is that, from the more specifically disciplinary point of view, there seems to be a crisis in the hierarchy of the elements which traditionally are associated with their typology (window display, sign, display space, point of purchase, decor for display and layout of the goods, spaces for facilities),

Functional design, associated with the phases of practice of consumerism, seems to have been completely subverted by the new values which inform these spaces. Even the materials and technologies no longer seems to respond solely to performance-related or functional requirements.

Research therefore follows two parallel tracks, that of the discipline which interprets design and its component elements, and that of cultural models which produce these elements and needs.

«The architecture of retail spaces must necessarily today take into account the economy of the production system and the fact that the retail outlet is no longer only a place for displaying and exhibiting goods but increasingly becomes its signifier context»[2].

The contemporary sales space is a place which integrates a multitude of spatial and functional aspects in a complex network crossed by systems of physical, social, cultural and economic relations which determine its character and specificity. It is the place in which material culture, business culture and the needs of the consumer become fully manifest through a complex system of synergies which comes into play between the specific ambits of the diverse spatial relations (material and immaterial). Consumer spaces are simultaneously places for the exchange of goods and symbolic and metaphorical territories.

Space not only takes on the task of showing goods and representing their value, but also interrelates with the customer who becomes the true protagonist and is no longer relegated to the role of spectator.

«The globalized post-industrial system is producing a commodity culture, in the sense that the goods system not only represents the most widespread economic medium in our society, but also expresses new individual moral values and logics, selective and complex values of profound social identities, as in the case of ethical consumption»[3].

---

[2] Mangiarotti, R., "Progettare il punto vendita", *Modo*, n. 178, marzo 1997, pp. 51-54.

[3] Branzi, A.,"Retailing in the globalization era", in AA.VV., *Places & Themes of Interiors Contemporary Research Worldwide*, Franco Angeli, Milano 2008.

2.2

the culture of design and the development of retail spaces

«Retail designers will have in the future to pay more heed to social-cultural aspects. Working in international contexts, with increasing globalization and mobility will challenge retail designers to give expression to 'local' values whilst retaining variation, flexibility and peace in an increasingly urban society»[1].

Since the 1980's, the design of retail space has once again become central to the profession, acting as interpreter for the changes in the economic and social structure and an experimental environment for the discipline of interior design, graphics and communication. Design used to be focused on production, aided by technology which made it possible to increase the sales area and the range of goods (as in the case of the escalator and air conditioning). Research on the relationship between consumers and purchasing experience have emphasised how the new centre of gravity of design would shift from goods to the customer.

---

[1] van Amerongen, R., Christiaans, H., *Retail & Interior Design*, Episode Publishers, 2004, p. 15.

The driving force behind this shift in focus, not only on the part of designers but first and foremost on the part of the companies, naturally arise from changes which must be traced back to the broader cultural, political and economic landscape. Now that material requirements have been satisfied, the consumer concentrates more on immaterial and psychological requirements, moving from *functional shopping* to *recreational shopping*.

According to Andrea Branzi, design culture:

«[...] still refer to the doctrinal fundaments suggested by Le Corbusier at the Athens Charter, 1933, where the new industrial city organism is proposed as segmented into specialized and separated area: Residence, Work, Industry. Leisure. However, one of the most apparent effects of the Third Industrial Evolution resides in the gradual disappearance of these separations and specialisations; the phenomenon of mass entrepreneurship, diffused work, capillary use of electronic and information instruments modified the operation of the city itself, internally and deeply, The city's architectural structures, once conceived for specialised functions on the basis of rational and sectional patters, are now used in a disparate, improper, temporary fashion: it is tendentially possible to carry out "any activity anywhere". This observation represent a brand-new subject for the Interior Design culture and opens a new season of design experimentation and deeper inspection into the new frontiers of an urban reality that not only needs to be continuously "re-functionalized" in order to give hospitality to unexpected activities, but also witnesses a contamination of the same business, residential and cultural activities. No more as separated environmental realities, but rather as active elements of an *enzymatic territory*, always changing its function and form»[2].

Design strategy is undergoing a transformation and the outcome is to create not only spaces and objects, but lines of intervention on reality, knowledge systems (Ikea does not only sell products with an excellent price-quality ratio, but also intervenes in the process of choice, culture

---

[2] Basso Peressut, L., Forino, I., Postiglione, G., Scullica, F., *Places and Themes of Interiors Reserach Worldwide*, Franco Angeli, Milano 2008, p. 96.

practice of consumption and spaces for goods

and habits). As Valeria Iannilli[3], says, the proof is to be found in the development of retail design which have undergone such a radical transformation as to require previously unknown skills. Design, closely interlinked with interior design, technological innovation, marketing, management, psychology, sociology, etc, plays a decisive role. Alongside design and other disciplines, there has been the emergence of a widespread, fluid, design culture entrusted to the consumers themselves. Retail spaces are starting to appear where the consumers play a design role both in terms of the space and that of the range of what is for sale. The consumer is no longer observed from the perspective of his expectations in terms of needs, wants and desires, but from the viewpoint of his being able to influence the entire consumer system.

> «It is necessary to understand that the sale space, recently seen as a place of experience, will be modified again in order to become a laboratory space where we are able to carry out some activities»[4].

Design for Retail will increasingly become the design of the possible relationship between the public and business, public and public, product and public.
When the focal point of the shop shifts from the goods to the customer, the designer needs to closely observe the customer, understand what expectations he has, what needs and feelings. Interior design is the exchanger which makes it possible to condition what is customary in the interrelations between people and their surroundings.

---

[3] Iannilli, V., *The Future of Retail Store Design*, in Basso Peressut, L., Forino, I., Postiglione, G., Scullica, F., *Places and Themes of Interiors Reserach Worldwide*, Franco Angeli, Milano 2008, p. 114.

[4] *Ibidem.*

2.3

the exploded project

practice of consumption and spaces for goods

The space of commerce is the synthesis of an *outside*, i.e. the surrounding in relation to the space, and of an *inside*, that is a place which is spatially organized. The aim of making the connection between product, customer and market, is pursued by the use of architectural devices.

The goals to be achieved are many and refer to very different categories: from a functional point of view it is necessary to organize movements and trajectories, make the choice of goods comfortable and quick, create environmental convenient microclimatic conditions. But it is necessary to build the customer's taste, too, create the market, suggest choice opportunities.

As we already pointed out many times in this treatise, the ways in which these goals are pursued have not only changed, but they are fragmented within a scenario continuously evolving. The present chapter takes into consideration four specific categories (*Identity*, *Shopwindow*, *Entrance*, *Display Apparel*), according to the classical hierarchy of the components of the project of the space of commerce, leaving out many others.

TAKE

McLEANS

AFTER MEALS

START TODAY
MAKE NO DELAY

2.3.1

IDENTITY

«Identity allows for the recognition of a continuity of attributes of form and content which go beyond differences which may be encountered on the plane of manifestation; that is, the presuppose for the persistence of an unvarying node which ensures the permanence of the object through its various forms »[1].

The concept of identity is closely linked to that of memory. The unvarying node, as Chirico defined it, is the set of basic values, the essentials, expressed in this case by the sales outlet capable of becoming independent of a context which is experiencing continuous change.

This set of characteristics, which refer back to complex expressive whole that includes constructive, exhibitive and communicative techniques, together represent recognition, an element of primary importance in building a relationship based on trust with the customer.

At the origins of the great retail outlets, the identity of the place was inseparable from the (good) name of the shopkeeper: from Macy's to Adolf Loos' shop Kniže, identity, quality and reliability were guaranteed by the name of the owner.

With the cancellation of the demarcation line between the manufacturer and the seller, and above all between the seller and owner of the retail outlet, this personal relationship lost any sense.

Until the 1980's, the complex mechanism of brand building replaced the physical personality of the shopkeeper. It was the brand that represented the identity, whether it was the name of a chain, a department store or a brand. The mechanism for translating this into the architectural field was to build recognition of the interiors which were intended to represent the quality of the brand and make it recognisable in all its

---

[1] Chirico, A. *Il successo comunicativo dei Diesel Stores* in Pezzini, I., Crivelli, P., a cura di, *Scene del consumo: dallo shopping al museo*, Meltemi, Roma, 2006.

forms and all four corners of the world. It was the chain store, with its pilot design where the materials, colours, lights and type of decor were laid down with fine precision in a sort of abacus of elements to then be replicated in each branch, a project which had already been explored in Le Corbusier's Bat'a.

It was not until the mid-1980's that a completely different approach would emerge in the experiment of Esprit.

It is true that the differentiation of one shop from another of the same brand had already been done by Robert Mallet-Stevens for Bally as well as by Shiro Kuramata for Issey Miyake[2] but the linguistic key of the designer persisted as an element of continuity, unvarying node.

Esprit was interested from the design viewpoint in exploring the different ways of outfitting a space using the range of expressive potential of designers: its retail outlets (offices and showrooms) were designed by some of the most influential names in the field of design, people like Norman Foster, Aldo Cibic, Shiro Kuramata, Terry Dwan, Ettore Sottsass and Antonio Citterio. This is the same approach adopted by Prada, almost twenty years later, with the design of different projects was commissioned to different studios like OMA, Herzog & De Meuron and Kazuyo Sejima + Ryue Nishizawa/Sanaa. This produced very different images within which the identity was more tied to a quest for innovation rather than any formal solution.

But the concept of identity, since it is so closely bound to that of the meaning of the message it wishes to communicate, proposes still more diverse interpretations such as that of Rei Kawakubo in Comme des Garçons who builds its identity around an image which is always changing, innovative, playing on the unpredictably and ironic criticism of the fashion establishment, in the conviction that the enthusiasm for *super architecture* only leads to a dead end.

---

[2] I refer to the *Progenitors'* projects chosen as representative for this study.

>>Freitag Flagshipstore, Zurigo, Spillmann Echsle
Architekten, 2006
The concept of the project reinforce the potential expressivity of recycled material, the textile
one used to cover up containers, transformed by Freitag in fashion bags; the building is
constructed with containers, to underline the sustainable approach.

>>Maison Martin Margiela

>>Camper

16| De Lairesse Pharmacy, Amsterdam, Concrete, 2002

2.3.2

JUDGE A BOOK FROM ITS COVER

The shop is a static mechanism having the primary task to attract costumers from a public outside place to the internal one of the exhibition of goods. It is the visit card defining the principles regulating the relationship between customer and shop, carrying messages, either inviting or refusing, telling about the product and suggesting how to use it.

The evolution of the role of shopwindows is worth a separate discussion[1], Here we wish to synthetically underline what are the different roles played by this element in the course of time.

From its first appearance at the end of '700 up to the beginning of '900, the task of the shopwindow was substantially to present the variety and the quantity of goods the shop could offer. Already at the end of '20 s, Robert Mallet-Stevens, with the Bally Shoe Shop project, expressly examines how to attract customers. The composition of the façade is always aimed to bring out the shopwindow, showing the new products and becoming the diaphragm dividing the road from the new architecture.

From '700, from the physical place, the diaphragm between buyer and seller with the precise role to present the sale object, the shopwindow turned out to be a means to draw the attention, apart from the presentation of goods. The function of visibility gradually shifted from the shopwindow to the shop inside, leaving outside the task to communicate messages going beyond the relationship with the product. Strategies are very different: from that used by Hans Hollein for Retti Candle Shop, where the shopwindow strongly stands out against the context and the relationship with the customer is stimulated by curiosity,

---

[1] See *Bibliography* for a selection of books on the subject.

to that of Selfridges in London, more recently. Selfridges is considered as the forerunner of dematerialization of the communicative role of the shopwindow with regard to the product. Its shopwindows are changed very often, showing actual *showcases,* in which every time artworks and installations about specific events or matters of particular social relevance are presented. The shop tells its opinion about the subjects which are interesting for the customers.

>>Malcolm Mc Laren, Sex, London

>>Selfridges, London, the shopwindow as an art piece

>> Diesel, Berlin, interactive windows, Liganova, 2009

>>Hermes, Tokyo, Tokujin Yoshioka, 2009

>>Balenciaga, London, 2008

2.3.3

ENTRANCE

The threshold, the relationship between the space perceived as public and the space protected of the shop, is one of the variables most influencing the typology of the link that the shop/brand wishes to establish not only with the potential customer but also with the whole city.

Tiffany & Co., the memorable jeweller's shop, in front of which Audrey Hepburn was day-dreaming in *Breakfast at Tifanny's*[1], points out its exclusivity by raising an actual barrier between the refinement of the internal environment, confidential and reserved to a few people, and the rest of the world outside. The entrance, closed by an armoured protection, turns the whole building into a safe. The presence of a watchman, controlling those who enter the shop, emphasizes even more the clear threshold between in and out.

The classical, symmetric, full and consistent façade emphasizes the relationship between full and empty with large transparent mirrors in the upper part both of shopwindows and fixture of the entrance. Thus, the big proportions of the inside are reflected in the outside, while the solemnity of the entrance is given by a flared frame with the impression of the name of the shop and the famous clock above it. On the contrary, the space useful for showing the goods is at a minimum, in other shops limited to actual niches within the façade. Tiffany has become a real touristic destination, the point of sale aims to feed the dream represented by the brand and not yet to advertise a specific product.

The general store Grayson's entrance, designed and built in 1941 in Seattle by Victor Gruen, is preceded by an area to create a new relationship with the road, de facto eliminating the line of demarcation between the public space of the road and that semi-private of the shop,

---

[1] *Breakfast at Tiffany's*, directed by Blake Edwards, 1961, from the novel by Truman Capote.

such as a promiscuous strip of passageway and commercial activity. The two shopwindow-isles, the windows and the depressed exhibition area create an articulated space de-materializing the place of threshold, the point of entrance between in and out. The extension of the shopwindow within the hall of the entrance leads to the shop inside without realizing it. The huge concave, yellow façade, supported by two big columns in copper colour, builds up the relationship of the building with outside and sets it as an interlocutor in urban scale, visible night and day, either on foot or by car.

The Olivetti Showroom of New York, designed by BBPR in 1954, differently uses a similar strategy providing a withdrawal of the shopwindow and entrance line in comparison with the road line, to acquire ad external space attracting passers-by to what can be defined as the antechamber of the shop. This external, public space is treated like an internal space, with a marble pavement and a counter-ceiling and with a display element, generated by the pavement, just like inside the shop. The transparent membrane of the shopwindow and the delimitation mark between the two different natures of spaces disappear.

The element entrance becomes a potential attractor. Through a trickery, the space of the shop prevails over the external space with one significant feature. At Comme des Garçons' in New York[2], the traditional façade in red bricks of an ex-industrial building, at the entrance of the shop, is matched against an element in stainless steel, apparently wishing to convey the passer-by into the shop.

---

[2] Comme des Garçon, Future System, New York 1988.

CHIARA
D'ESTE
SHOW-ROOM

1ª PIANO

MAISⓃN
MARTIN

MARGIELA

few different examples of how the interior space of the shop relates to the exterior public space:

>>Tiffany, New York
The relationship between public and private space is strongly divided through a barrier to underline the exclusivity of the interior.

>>Grayson, Seattle, Victor Gruen
The relationship between public and private space is mediated by an indeterminate area that tends to cancel the threshold.

>>Showroom Olivetti, New York, BBPR
One element from the commercial space, invades the public space to play the catalyst role.

>>Comme des Garçons, New York, Future Systems
The element that from the inside communicate with the outside is very small but very strong from a linguistic point of view.

2.3.4

DISPLAY SETTING

The principle adopted to display the goods, defined as *visual merchandising*, is another means to communicate the relevant context of goods.

The equipment to display goods is turning into a concept of global setting, remodelling materials, tools and technologies from other sectors. The most evident comparison you can draw is the one with *exhibition design*. Albini, in the project of Zanini Furrier's had shown how it was possible to mediate the *display setting* through the tools belonging to *exhibition design*.

For the reasons mentioned in the previous chapters, the setting of the shop, the exhibitors and the way the product is emphasized are often more important than the product sold.

One variable which substantially altered the project approach is the one of the life cycle of the point of sale. In the *temporary store*, display equipment, which can either be linguistically transparent or very characterized, have a very short life in common. The *temporary store* is being successful as a winning typology also as a flexible solution to the fluctuations of demand, which are more and more unforeseeable. The necessity of having reversible elements gave new life to the seek for an equilibrium between initial investment and communicative result. The continuous experimentation of materials and non-conventional equipment (we refer to typologies of hanging stands and set of shelves), which the most interesting contemporary projects share in common, creates an endless abacus of solutions hardly able to be attributed to a specific scope of the project.

two examples on how the display setting can the focus of the layout project

>>Marni, London, Future Systems, 1999
The display setting, together with the clothes, is the main point of the project; it's a sculpture concept and even the hangers are especially designed.

>>Mandarina Duck, Paris, Droog Design + NL Architects
Droog Design together with NL Architects defined the store they designed as «a store without architecture» (da Barreneche, R. A., *New Retail*, Phaidon Press, London 2005, p. 185). The display setting is characterized by exhibition objects with a strong communication value: the Pin Wall, an aluminium structure to fit bags a little objects just pushing pins mounted on a grid and the Rubber Wall were goods are kept in place by big rubber bands; the shop closed down on February 2003 after only 28 month of opening.

some of the display setting's equipment relate to both linguistic and functional issues

>>Prada Epicentre, OMA, Los Angeles, 2004

and other just responding to communicative intent through the experimentation of new materials or unusual settings

>>Apple Store di Issey Miyake, Erwan e Ronan Bouroullec, Paris, 2000

typology of temporary shop gives the occasion to experiment non conventional materials ad equipment; even communication is no more based on stability, usually spatially represented by the use of precious materials but, on the opposite, is creativity and surprise to pay a major role.

>>Me Issey Miyake, Curiosity-Nicolas Gwenael, 2001

>>Foot Soldier, Wonderwall, Tokyo, 2001

>>Areaware + Charles & Marie + I.D. Magazine, Design Miami 2008, Rich Brilliant Willing

>>Shop & Show Pop-up, Tracey Neuls, London, 2009

2.4

progenitors

The final chapter in this section focuses on the *progenitors*.

12 design projects between 1905 and 2004 which mark 12 landmark stages in the ideas, designs, and story of what it was firmly believed that space should represent.

Each of the designers, among the biggest names on the international scene, not only came up with a design which was highly innovative in a number of different ways, but also made a great contribution in terms of theory and research, expressing an original point of view in the field of design in the context of retail space.

Adolf Loos, in addition to being one of the masters of Modernism and designing more than one shop, also wrote essays on (men's) fashion which define the personality of his designs, too often only linked to the concept of practical architecture, without any useless decorations, completely separate from any idea of art.

Between 1928 and 1930, two design projects were the expression of two new types of retail space: Robert Mallet-Stevens worked on a series of projects for the footwear brand Bally, giving each one a particular character all its own while building a theoretical compendium on the meaning of the shop as a window display for the new architecture. And two years later, Dudok produced a design project for the De Bijenkorf department store in Rotterdam. The building and its interiors, destroyed in the bombings during the Second World War, was the architectural and conceptual epitome of what these microcosms represented in the city.

With his Bat'a design which was never built, Le Corbusier went one step further in his theory of functionalism, foreseeing the concept of coordinated image which would shortly become so commonplace. In Italy, we move forward to 1945 and the Post-War period and a project by Franco Albini, representative of what was best in Italian design culture which questioned interior design instruments. Hans Hollein, with his 1965 design for the Retti candle shop was the first to explicitly introduce the emotional concept: the shop was designed to attract the customer and arouse curiosity and more strictly functional aspects were relegated to a secondary position. Shiro Kuramata, who was described by Giò Ponti's Domus as «very good»[1], was the one who for the very first time, or maybe just better than others, experimented with the use of materials which were not normally associated with interior design, turning the image of the retail space on its head and opening the way for many subsequent projects.

The case of Esprit is represented by the work of Sottsass Associati in 1986, where Memphis is tamed down passing through art galleries and a design for a functional space. The shop for Katharin Hamnett designed in 1987 by Norman Foster does not even have a display window. It is inside a courtyard and introduces for the first time the reuse of industrial fixtures and fittings in retail design. In 1996, Calvin Klein commissioned the young architect John Pawson to design its flagship store in New York: the *minimal* style of the shop reflected that of the designer's clothing and this was the first of many artistic marriages which would see a

---

[1] "Shiro Kuramata: due negozi a Tokyo", *Domus*, n. 493, December 1970.

merging of these two expressive languages. Beginning with Pawson, it ended with OMA's Prada New York where the shop became something other than itself in a quest for contamination from other building types. The design project, or perhaps I should say projects, with which I have chosen to close this selection of *progenitors*, is that of Guerrilla Stores for the Comme des Garçons brand with the designer Rei Kawakubo at the helm. I am closing with the only one who was not an architect (or designer), whose insight into space were so influential that the Harvard Design School of Design awarded her the Harvard Excellence in Design Award in 2000 and dedicated an exhibition to her work with the title Structure + Expression Comme des Garçons[2].

These 12 case studies represent landmark moments in design culture, not only for their own period, but for the influence they had on design projects which came after, as *progenitors*.

---

[2] The exhibition has been held at the Gund Hall Gallery, May 4-31, 2000.

2.4.1

ADOLF LOOS, THE KNIŽE SHOP, WIEN, 1910-13

In 1898, Adolf Loos wrote an article on male fashion for the *Neue Freie Press* introducing the concept of *understatment*[1].

«What does being well dressed mean? It means being dressed properly!»[2].

This statement, which on the one part was coherent with the line of thought which characterised the writings and works of Adolf Loos also added a new critical variable: the inflexible dictats of the essay *Ornament und Verbrechen*[3] against the use of ornament in architecture, which makes a clear distinction between it and the discipline of art, are softened somewhat by the discovery of the particular attention which Loos devotes to the world of fashion.

Speaking about his customers, the tailors Goldman and Salatsch, we discover a true dandy, who indubitably exerted considerable influence with his attention to the design of retail space:

«This excellent person – in reality they were two excellent fellows – had, year after year, made clothes for me and patiently forwarded me his bill every first of January, a bill which, I must confess, was never less than the year before. Notwithstanding the manner in which my benefactors fiercely denied the accusation, I still cannot but suspect that this flattering assignment was given to me because in some small way, in this way, the bill was reduced»[4].

---

[1] Loos, A., "La moda Maschile" in *Neue Freie Presse*, a viennese magazine founded by Adolf Werthner, Max Friedländer and Michael Etienne in 1864, published until 1938.

[2] Loos, A., *Ins Leere Gesprochen 1897-1900*, Georges Crès, Paris 1921, trad it. *Parole nel vuoto*, Adelphi, Milano 1972, p.11.

[3] Loos, A., *Ornament und Verbrechen*, Innsbruck 1908, Vienna 1930, trad. it. "Ornamento e delitto", *Casabella Continuità* 233, novembre 1959, pp. 39-40.

[4] Loos, A., *Ins Leere Gesprochen 1897-1900*, Georges Crès, Paris 1921, trad it. *Parole nel vuoto*, Adelphi, Milano 1972, p. 233.

During his career, Loos dealt with the theme of retail space in nearly thirty projects. His interest in the sector crosses the boundaries of what is strictly speaking interior design to take on broader issues such as that of distribution and the role of the shopkeeper, the one who by a process of selection, educates the taste of the customer through the product range:

«A new type of shop is represented by *tailors* and *outfitters*. The *outfitter* stocks everything connected with gentlemen's clothing. His task is no easy one. For each article he stocks, he must be able to guarantee that it will have the effect of making him more gentlemanlike. One expects in a well managed clothing shop to be able have blind faith that one incurs no risk of leaving with a garment in bad taste. The gentleman's *outfitter* can make no concession to common taste. A quality shop need never resort to the sort of justifications which must satisfy the tastes of all to some extent. This means he may never make a mistake. Should he, by any chance, make a mistake, he has a duty towards his customers to immediately get rid of the article in question. It is difficult to reach the role of guide in the field of fashion, but it is even more difficult to keep this position. And yet, only a fraction of the articles on sale are made in the outfitter's workshop. First and foremost, he is a salesman. In his dealings with the craftsmen, he behaves like the owner of an art gallery does with an artist. The gallery owner too must choose only the best of the entire production. Something which involves enough commitment to fill a lifetime [...] I am no detective. The origin of the goods is a matter of complete indifference to me. The main point is that the shopkeeper be able to supply certain goods, tailored in a certain manner»[5].

The shop design of the Kniže gentleman's outfitters in Vienna (official supplier to the Empire) was a forerunner of the later one in Berlin in 1924 and the Paris outlet in 1927.
As is clear from this design, Adolf Loos did not believe that retail interior design should respond to requirements very different from those of interior design in the domestic environment. The real difference is that the relationship with the exterior, with the street, becomes a central

---

[5] *Ibidem*, pp. 93-94.

and functional element in the design. The facade of the Kniže shop, with its black granite standing out against the white building, creates a frame for the display window, assigning it a strong communicative role.

The interior is laid out over two floors: the ground floor is a very small space where there is the entrance lobby and the stairway which leads to the first floor. The first floor houses the showrooms and is where the goods are on display. The connotations of the space recall the *English gentlemen's club* with fireplaces and conversation spaces and the use of the finest materials and finishes, so that these rooms are cosy and welcoming, a place where not only can the customer buy garments of the finest quality but he can also pass the time in an aristocratic setting.

>>Adolf Loos, The Kniže Shop, Vienna, 1910-13
The small entrance on the ground floor hosts on the two walls the drawers with accessories and the staircase leading to the first floor. The stair is central to the design, in bended wood has a mirror panelling to permit visual communication in between ground and first floor.
At the first floor space to choose textiles and models; the first room at the arrival of the stair has a wooden false ceiling; the other rooms have very high ceiling and a mezzanine.

>>Goldman & Salatsch, Wien, Adolf Loos, 1909-1911
The display setting is organized on the lateral walls and around the pillars, with glass equipment. In the basement, the sportswear department, a big staircase lead to the mezzanine where is place the administrative department, the cash desk and the textile showroom.

2.4.2

ROBERT MALLET STEVENS, BALLY SHOES SHOP, PARIS, 1928

Mallet-Stevens, in the mid-1920's, designed a number of retail spaces. His experience of designing spaces for a large number of small clients, then for Alfa Romeo, Peugeot and Bally, contributed to the development of a critical theory geared towards the typology and role that this architecture was acquiring in the culture of the modern city.

Some years later, Le Corbusier would produce one shop design which would constitute the opportunity to develop and general theory of retail design.

In the course of numerous conferences, articles and interviews, Mallet-Stevens stressed how shop architecture was one of the main areas of experimentation in the new architecture. The theme of retail space translated into the possibility of giving shape to a vivid image of the contemporary city and presented an opportunity for its renewal.

«No modern day shop owner would dare build a shop inspired by the styles of the past. All retail space built in recent times is modern […] An Louis XIV automobile showroom or a ... Outlet in the style of Napoleon III would be met with hilarity. The eye of the passerby is used to modern lines and proportions. In France, modern art has followed this strange path: theatrical backdrops, retail space, advertising posters, architecture – while in other countries, it has been architecture that has driven the process of renewal […] It is the passerby, enthusiastic about the shops, who will produce the most effective propaganda for modern building; his eye, used to the new proportions, judicious lighting, logical lines, will soon be unable to tolerate the dusty canopies, narrow windows and dirt-blackened mouldings»[1].

---

[1] R. Mallet-Stevens, "Le Décor de la rue, Préface de Présentation", in *Parade*, n. 37, janvier 1930, cit. in C. Volpi, *Robert Mallet-Stevens 1886-1945*, Electa, Milano 2005, p. 207-208.

The characteristics of the modern shop encompass both its exterior and interior image. Above all, it plays a specific role as an element of urban design and advertising poster. The interiors must highlight the products, as if they were theatrical backdrops and must reflect the modern character of the goods.

«In France, modern art has followed this strange path: theatrical backdrops, retail space, advertising posters, architecture – while in other countries, it has been architecture that has driven the process of renewal. The dancer and the shopkeeper have been understood (let us thank them, congratulate them), had the felicitous idea of starting a movement which should benefit all; a new era begins; air, light, joy [...] It is the passerby, enthusiastic about the shops, who will produce the most effective propaganda for modern building»[2].

In the lecture he gave in 1930 at the École Boulle, which was published in the magazines *Parade*[3] and *Magasins et Bureaux*[4], Mallet-Stevens further explained his ideas on the advertising role of the shop: the window display is an essential element because it is the medium through which a relationship is established with the customer. The lighting, the location of the shop and the presentation of the products are other decisive factors. Retail space must attract customers with its materials, colours, light and shapes or with the products its presents.

His approach to design was diametrically opposed to that of Adolf Loos and had more in common with Hoffman's idea of an integration of art, fashion and architecture.

---

[2] Mallet-Stevens, R., "Préface", *Le décor de la rue, les magasins, les étalages, les stands d'exposition, les éclairages*, Les Éditions de Parade, Paris 1929, pp. 3-4.

[3] "Le magasin et le décor de la rue. Conférence faite par M. R. Mallet-Stevens devant les élèves de l'École Boulle", *Parade*, n. 27, 15 marzo 1929, p. 10, *Parade*, n. 28, 15 aprile 1929, p. 9; *Parade*, n. 29, 15 maggio 1929, p. 7; *Parade*, n. 30, 15 giugno 1929, p. 12; *Parade*, n. 31, 15 luglio 1929, p. 9; *Parade*, n. 32, 15 agosto 1929, pp.8-9.

[4] Mallet-Stevens, R., "L'art de la Rue. La Rue et les Magasins modernes. Conditions d'établissement du plan et de la façade d'un Magasin", *Magasins et bureaux*, n. 44, luglio 1930, pp. 19-23; *Magasins et bureaux*, n. 46, ottobre 1930, pp. 7-11; *Magasins et bureaux*, n. 47, novembre 1930, pp. 11-17.

«In the outfitting of retail spaces, it is good that fashion, which has no alliance to the field of art, be present [...] 'a shop in which everything is fashion, must adapt to the movement. The goods are transformed for no apparent reason: the surroundings must do the same and the consequent renewal of the street gives the city an intense vitality. A shop may be treated in an architectural manner (style), but must present decorative details (fashion). In any case, the shop signs must always be fashionable, if possible, actually be ahead of the trend»[5].

Mallet-Stevens is also innovative in terms of his design methodology which envisaged close collaboration with the other designers and tradesmen in the sector.

After his experience designing a hat shop and the headquarters of Madame Paquin in New York during the pre-War years, he was commissioned by the designer Melnott-Simonin and the costume designers Muelle and Rossignol to outfit a showroom and a gallery where they could present their designs.

1925 was the year in which he became involved in the design project for the Alfa Romeo workshop garage and showroom in boulevard Haussmann and rue Marbeuf in Paris. By the time he designed the Peugeot showroom in the Champs-Élysées, he seemed to have applied fully the principles of that lecture at the École Boulle.

His work for Bally involved not only three shops in Paris in boulevard de la Madeleine, rue de Ternes and boulevard des Capucines, but also three other shops (the one in Lyons in 1930, Rouen in 1934 and Algiers in 1937) e constituted his major achievement in the field of retail design. The shop in boulevard de la Madeleine was the first in the series. The shop facade, applied onto that of the pre-existing 19th century building, was notable for its covering in metal panels which created a layered effect of horizontal lines. The goods were displayed in a long display cabinet with gilt bronze edging at eye level, which protruded slightly from the facade. The sign was a metal strip with gilt letters and in terms of composition, created a link between the window display and

---

[5] C. Volpi, *Robert Mallet-Stevens 1886-1945*, Electa, Milano 2005, p. 208-209.

the entrance and above it there was a cantilevered lighting strip which separated the shop front from the upper floors of the building.

The facade was an element which served to heighten the recognizability of shop, unifying some architectural elements without standardising the type as Le Corbusier would later do in his Bat'a design.

In keeping with Mallet-Stevens' conviction mentioned above of the necessity of collaboration with other professionals and specific tradesmen, as far as the outfitting of the interior was concerned, Francis Jourdain was put in charge of designing the furnishings, Andrè Salomon was responsible for lighting, and Hélène Henry was in charge of upholstery.

>>Interiors of Bally Shop Bally, Paris, 1929

>>Facade of the Bally Shop Paris, 1929

>>Bally shop, boulevard de la Madeleine, Paris, 1928

>>Peugeot, Robert Mallet-Stevens, 1929

22| De Bijenkorf,1930, exterior (picture©KLM Aerocarto)

2.4.3

WILLEM M. DUDOK, DE BIJENKORF, ROTTERDAM, 1930

De Bijenkorf, literally the beehive, opened in 1870 with a small store in Niewwendijk, one of the oldest streets in Amsterdam, but within a few years it would turn into on of the most prestigious Dutch department store chains.

I deemed it necessary to include a case study of a department store in this section on *progenitors*, since it is such a fascinating building type, and has had such an influence on consumer habits, providing retail design with new and specific design ideas.

The Rotterdam project saw Willem Marinus Dudok involved in the creation of a building which was the exact expression of both the requirements of the contractor and the architectural ideas of its times, while including those personal details which, somewhat later, led to the term *dudoky* being coined to describe the many buildings around the United States and Europe which so blatantly imitated his style[1].

Largely thanks to the magazine *Wendingen*[2] a fair number of images have survived to give us a clear idea of the interiors and details of the building which was completely destroyed during the bombings of the Second World War.

De Bijenkorf reopened on the same site in 1955 built to a design by Marcel Breuer.

From 1916 onwards, Dudok was the town architect in the small town of Hilversum near Amsterdam, where he dealt with various aspects of urban design and designed several projects among which the famous

---

[1] In 1931 engineer Van der Steur wrote: «Our time is still without a style. And in the place of style, fashion takes over [...] Dudok himself knows better than us that after the fashion of the "School of Amsterdam" it arrived the "Dudok fashion"», in Casciato, M., "W. M. Dudok. Il municipio di Hilversum 1923-1931, in *Domus*, n. 680, February 1987, p. 60.

[2] Wendingen (Inversions) is a monthly art review published in between 1918 and 1932.

town hall in 1928-30, a contemporary of the De Bijenkorf design.

He grew up in the Berlaghian tradition, but his style would appear to have owed more to the major figure of Frank Lloyd Wright, especially to the Prairie Houses and the Larkin Building, from which he took and reinterpreted in his own way the asymmetrical composition of rectangular blocks and the use of exterior brickwork. Although little studied in the field of modern advertising, Dudok received a number of awards during his lifetime, including the RIBA Gold Medal (1935), the French Grand Prix of architecture (1937) and the AIA Gold Medal (1955).

In August 1928, he was commissioned to design the building in Rotterdam. According to the author, the architectural container was supposed to act as an advertisement. With its 137,000 square metres, the new De Bijenkorf was one of the largest and most modern department stores in Europe and as well as retail space, restaurants and facilities,

>>De Bijenkorf, 1930, the restaurant

practice of consumption and spaces for goods

23| De Bijenkorf, Marcel Breuer, Rotterdam, interior;

Marcel Breuer, in collaboration with Jaap Elzas, designed the new building for De Bijenkorf that was completed in 1957. The building, organized in five stories and the basement, has a facade characterised by a panelling in travertino (Italian marble), with small vertical windows; last floor, that hosts the offices and the restaurant, has big windows and skylights. The structure has beamless reinforced-concrete floor with concrete pillars away the one from the other twelve meters. The layout is organized around the stairs, the elevator and the central escalator. The building still looks the same today but the interiors have been heavily modified nevertheless few original details can be still seen.

2.4.4

LE CORBUSIER, BAT'A, PROJECT, 1935

The design by Le Corbusier for Bat'a represents an exceptional case, a synthesis of a whole series of considerations which influenced the way in which shops were designed up until a few years ago.

The standardization and prefabrication of systems and components has always been, at least from a certain point onwards, one of the focal points of research into retail building design.

As in the other cases selected in this study, for Corbusier too, design went hand in hand with an explicit idea of what the retail space should represent. Within the broader vision of Le Corbusier, which make him one of the greatest architects of all time, retail is dealt with as the «scientific and natural digestion of the customer», a definition which seems to have met with the agreement of both the designer and Mr. Bat'a[1].

With a very different approach from that used by Adolf Loos for the Kniže gentlemen's outfitters, the formula for the Bat'a shops was based on the quick sale. The shop constitutes a nodal point in metropolitan traffic and consumption has picked up speed as it has grown in volume, delegating to the shop the role of a *machine* for capturing flows and selling products.

---

[1] Le Corbusier, *Œuvre complète de 1910-1929*, Les éditions d'architecture Erlanbach, Zurich 1948, p. 157.
«La vente est rigoureusement la contrepartie de la fabrication. Dans une entreprise mondiale comme celle de Bat'a, la vent droit s'opérer avec un sécurité mathématique. Le boutiques sont dans les villes, les village, les bourgs, partout. Elles dont minuscules, moyennes ou très vastes. Les problème: attirer l'attention du passant; l'arrêter dans la rue, lui montrer un choix étonnant d'articles; lui faire pousser la porte de la boutique presque inconsciemment; le faire s'asseoir, lui inspirer une immense confiance par la profusion des articles, la rapidité du service; puis, avant qu'il arrive à la caisse, avoir soumis sa curiosité et a sa convoitais quantité des petits articles accessoires...Il paie, il s'en va heureux d'être bien servi et d'avoir, d'un coup, pu se revitaliser en petit articles, qu'en temps normal on ne sait où aller chercher...Tout cela, et dans ses moindres détails, pendant deux heures, Jean Bat'a, le chef, a tenu à l'expliquer à Le Corbusier, afin que celui-ci l'aide à accomplir bien cette nécessité vitale: vendre [...]»

«For shops all around the world, where Bat'a will grow and develop, the standard which generates unity, diversity, efficiency, cheapness. Build proper shops but shops that are neither refined nor distinguished. Bat'a is realistic. He only wants the working class customer. The second aspect of the problem is, beyond the entrance door, the interior. The elements are: the shelving (casiers), the small display cases, the seating, the cash desk. In addition, a fundamental element, in the Bat'a shop, is the pedicure area (at the end of the store), A traffic problem, after all, and the establishment of standard dimensions. Any problems concerning standards causes and multiplies difficulties. What is possible, admissible, tolerable, in a thousand individual cases, becomes inadmissible in a problems of standards. Once a solution has been found, everything seems more simple, natural and spontaneous»[2].

The entire project was based on the stereometric model of the shoe box (11x15x30cm): the shop window is seen as a portal through which the public is *sucked*[3], , laid out according to fifteen types depending on the depth of the shopfronts and their breadth; the composition of the facade, always based on the same model, can be based on three basic designs, the one constant being the height of the entrance.

While Mendelsohn and Mallet-Stevens theorised in a concrete or abstract manner on the subject of retail space without defining any real methodological approach but experimenting in every new design project, Le Corbusier with systematic clarity was defining and resolving the problems of *machines for selling*: the identity of the brand is delegated to standardisation. This idea was the product of material culture which, with its clear and stereometric organisation, considers the process of selling to be on a par with the production line in a celebration of the product of the industrial process.

---

[2] Le Corbusier, *Œuvre complète de 1910-1929*, Les éditions d'architecture Erlanbach, Zurich 1948, p. 117-118.

[3] *Aspiré* is the term used in the drawing n. 3393. Interesting to underline how Rem Koolhaas used the concept of the *sucking porch* in the design of Prada Bevery Hills.

2.4.5

FRANCO ALBINI, PELLICCERIA ZANINI, MILANO, 1945

«The inventiveness of the display must draw the visitor into its game... the architecture must mediate between the public and the works displayed»[1].

Franco Albini one of the undisputed masters of the *interior design*, tradition and the epitome of that «artistic rationalism» described by Edoardo Persico[2], concentrated in his work on the outfitting, an element halfway between the decor and the supports, which served to organise the layout in domestic, exhibition or retail interiors.

Both the design project for Pellicceria Zanini furriers and the one for the bookshop Libreria Baldini & Castoldi fall within the context of the period just after the Second World War when Milan was in ruins but already in the process of being rebuilt.

Both projects, but especially the one for the furriers, given the particular nature of the goods involved, are distinguished by a measured, balanced approach in the layout, a seductive but restrained elegance, conscious of the post-war climate.

The approach adopted, the use of outfitting and materials coined from the context of exhibitions, is what is most distinctive about this design. The long narrow space of Pellicceria Zanini, divided by three curtains, is laid out as a series of three functional spaces. the first, the window display, with the crucial role of displaying the product to the outside; the second is the reception area, the space for trying on furs; the third space is for the service areas,

«The area devoted to display, rather than giving an image of conspicuous luxury which the theme might well have implied, aims to 'arrange' the objects on display, as if they were in a catalogue»[3].

---

[1] G. Celant, *Nizzoli*, Edizioni Comunità, Milano 1968, p. XIV-XV.

[2] Persico, E., "Un interno a Milano", *La Casa Bella*, n. 6, June 1932,

[3] Crespi, L., *Design e cultura tecnologica*, Poli.design, Milano 2005.

The inner skin is composed of a parquet floor laid in the traditional herringbone pattern, a soffit and vertical panelling which serves as the display space. The soffit is made of white wooden lists which stand out against a black background, also used as a support for fixing the lamps which hang by fine metal round bars. The walls are covered with alternating panels: frames of painted wood within which the goods are displayed, mirrors and panels of perforated wood from which drawings and fashion plates are hung. The furnishing are plain tables and armchairs made of metal round bars covered in black velvet.

The *lesson* that Albini contributed to interior design was the value of lightness and reversibility, as opposed to stability, which has had a lasting influence on retail design.

24| D Retti Candle Shop, exterior (picture©C. Cossa)

2.4.6

HANS HOLLEIN, RETTI CANDLE SHOP, WIEN, 1965

The way Hans Hollein, one of the cutting edge exponents of Postmodern architecture, does his projects is described as radical by Charles Jencks[1].

The little shop, which occupies a surface area of 16 square metres expresses the culture of rupture of the 70's and represents a culture which upsets all of the references of the culture of the project.

The project, with a new and diametrically opposed vision to all those exhibited up until now, expresses an approach more linked to the emerging world of design. It is as if the shop were an object dilated on the scale of architecture. The interior, as Gianni Pattena points out, is a conceptual and emotional place[2] and its organization, albeit in a very modest space, expresses a strong character.

The approach to the project is first of all determined by the relationship that he wants to establish with the exterior and the customer. Attention is drawn to the auto-referential architecture, by a window and by an interior which displays few items all of which have a dense significance. The exterior and interior are one and the same, continuity, highlighted by the use of materials, aluminium, used both inside and out in all the component parts of the shop. The interior display, which divides the space into two areas, separated only by narrowing, is the same on all its walls. The customer is put in direct contact with the goods without any mediation. Passing through the exhibition area, one accesses the warehouse area where one can proceed with the purchase.

The same approach in design was re-proposed by Hollein in

---

[1] Jencks, C., *The Language of Postmodern Architecture*, Rizzoli International, New York 1977.

[2] Pattena, G., *Hans Hollein, opere 1960-1988*, Ideabooks, Milano 1988, pp. 27-28.

some subsequent projects (like that of the Christa Metek shop or for Schullin I and II) ultimately defining little by little a linguistic character which will be reinterpreted by other designers.

>>Retti Candle Shop, Hans Hollein, 1965

>>Schullin II, Hans Hollein, 1982

2.4.7

SHIRO KURAMATA, MARKET ONE & SHOP ONE, TOKYO, 1970

Shiro Kuramata is one of the most refined and influential designers in modern Japan. His work is a synthesis of Japanese decorative art and design culture in which context Ettore Sottsass is considered to be one of his masters.

All of Kuramata's designs, from the very beginning, were permeated with a desire to defy gravity, to create spaces and furnishings that float. He pursues this idea by making use of transparent materials like glass, acrylic, metal mesh, pure materials often borrowed from a repertoire which has no connection whatsoever with the tradition of interior design and has a genuine passion for the possibilities offered by new technologies.

Market One and Shop One, published in Domus in 1970, were two shops in the same building, the Edwards Building in Tokyo. Market One, which has much in common in terms of approach with Hans Hollein, was conceived as an object inserted into a building: the front, completely transparent, reveals the continuous shell of the interior, made entirely of shiny white acrylic. In order to emphasise this ambition to *float*, the floor is a platform made of rubber and steel and is independent of the vertical structure. The furnishings are part of the shell itself and impressions made in the wall form the seating where «you can take refuge, as if you were inside a shell, in order to find yourself again».

In Shop I, the walls are also white and made of acrylic. The entire layout of the interior is based on the contrast of the white wall covering with the rows of holes housing chrome-plated pipes, all identical, which support glass shelves or clothes hooks which have a dual decorative and functional role. Shiro Kuramata has designed many shops for the brilliant Japanese designer Issey Miyake and his design output has always teetered on the borderline between the disciplines of interior design, outfitting and design with a multidisciplinary approach which immediately won over the design world and the critics who called him «very good»[1].

>>Issey Miyake Seibu, Tokyo, Shiro Kuramata, 1987
The boutique is inside the Seibu department store, realized in metal sheet, has a surface of 70 square meters.

---

[1] It's the last line of "Shiro Kuramata: due negozi a Tokyo" in *Domus*, n. 493, December 1970.

2.4.8

SOTTSASS ASSOCIATI, ESPRIT, KÖLN, 1986

At the beginning of 80's, Doug Tomkins, president of Esprit Holding, decides to transform to image of all spaces of the group. He chooses Sottsass Associati to interpret this renewal for the German shops and showroom.

The Cologne shop means letting Memphis theories cope with a functional context. Up to then, this group of avant-garde designers had been carrying out only concept and exhibition projects.

Esprit proves that the maturity of language had reached such a level to allow its organization into a spatial division. In the shop, the prevailing element is that of colours, choice of materials and original language. It is divided into three levels: the entrance is at the middle floor, where a gangway acts as a liaison, emphasizing the entrance into the space of the innovative brand for the access to the actual shop.

The gallery of the basement is not accessible to public and here there are facilities and offices, while the shop continues at the 1st floor. The linking element to the divided space is represented by the staircase-sculpture. The treatment of surfaces is particularly emphasized. Both the walls and the pavement of the shop are tiled in seminato, the stairs are in pink marmorino and the furniture is of a perfect Memphis style. The display equipment, aimed to organize the whole sales-space, is made of customized pieces of furniture, which, turning over the conventional scale proportions, thus achieve an architectural status.

«What is important in the Cologne Esprit showroom is not the image but the division of paths, the rough edges and the rarefaction of cut shapes, the harshness of edges, the autonomy of territories [...] The cutting and the delimitation of spaces through matters and colours let the assembly and the division of functions arise, bound to anatomical differences and the commodity sectors. The architecture of dressing turned out to be the dressing of architecture»[1].

The cooperation with Esprit will last some more years with other realizations and will be interrupted only because the Esprit policy wanted to associate its dressing line not to a stylistic key but to a continuous experimentation.

>>Sottsass Associati, Esprit, Köln, 1986

---

[1] Celant, G., *Domus*, n. 675, October 1986.

2.4.9

NORMAN FOSTER, KATHARIN HAMNETT, LONDON,1987

Norman Foster's project for Katharin Hamnett is one of the first examples of a refunctionalization by conversion of an industrial building, not having an access from the road, into a clothing shop.

The location of this boutique is an old workshop at Brompton Road, close to Michelin Building, renovated by Conran.

The project approach by Norman Foster is strictly bound to the interpretation of the features of the brand to be represented: elegance and refinement made by purity and simplicity.

One of the features of the space is to be within a courtyard and not to have a shopwindow onto the road. What can apparently be a problem turns out to be one of the main elements of enhancement, making this project the first of many others to come. The radical choice consists in not even setting any signs on the road: a glass catwalk is illuminated from below with neon lights, crosses the building and directly leads to the shop inside. The original nature of the internal space was kept: the industrial matrix was emphasized and enhanced by preserving its main elements.

The space is wide, apparently void, illuminated by the natural light of the large skylights. Dresses are concentrated on one side, nearly set apart. The impression of the natural light coming from the coverage was integrated by a system of artificial light above the coverage simulating the natural source. The pavement is in smoothed concrete and the few pieces of furniture (cases and windows) are in transparent glass, emphasizing the *stripping* and removal of any useless element. The linguistic approach of this shop, increasing the value of goods through an elegant and neutral environment, conceptually opens the way to the successive Pawson's work, who will implement, with his noble furniture and care of details, what has then be defined as *minimal* style.

>>Norman Foster, Katharin Hamnett, London,1987

2.4.10

JOHN PAWSON, CALVIN KLEIN, NEW YORK, 1995

Calvin Klein was the first important project for John Pawson and sealed a long collaboration between him and the American fashion designer.

This shop on Madison Avenue in New York, was fundamental for at least two reasons. The first is that it expressed a new language, later dubbed as *minimal*, which puts at the centre of the project a very simple articulation of the spaces, a rarefaction of the components, great attention to the solution of details and the selection of materials, for the most part precious. Secondly because it inaugurates, in the mid 90's a vein of collaboration which sees the most famous fashion designers associating their names with the most important designers in the world. The success of the so called flagshipstore, the shop which has the role of communicating the identity of the brand, has been one of the foremost phenomena in design in recent years, producing a great multitude of shops and buildings for commercial use characterized by a great experimental vein.

One of the first reflections of John Pawson, regarding the components of space for commerce, concerned the role and significance of the goods. It is not the goods, or indeed their quantity, that is able to capture the curiosity of the customers, which are dwindling in Calvin Klein shops, but rather the space that plays the starring role, expression of a symbolic value, able to represent, in and of itself, the concept of the brand. As Deyan Sudjic maintains, «it was the department stores that determined how Klein looked to his costumers»[1].

The ample interior and double height, which before had been occupied by the headquarters of a bank was completely revolutionised by Pawson who introduced a second floor. The new floor is however very

---

[1] Sudjic, D., *John Pawson: works*, Phaidon, London 2000, p.55.

withdrawn compared to the line of the facade so as to maintain the perception of a monumental space. All of the layout, which organizes the space into sections, was designed to minimize the impact of the pillars. Each section hosts a specific category of goods, reflecting a simple and efficient organization.

The prospect on the street is a sheet of glass which acts so that all of the shop becomes a window. The stairs that ascends to the first floor divides the shop into two areas in which the stone counters which the shop assistants need to show off the clothes seem to float. The floors are made of light yellow Yorkshire stone and the clothes are housed in niches, illuminated from above as if they were also a structural part of the space.

This first pilot store, consolidated a collaboration that has give rise to many other projects. John Pawson is more than a designer for Calvin Klein, he is almost an artistic director, able to interpret and enhance the brand, make it recognizable, in its distinctive features, managing to differentiate the language, according to the diverse contexts and various types of commercial space.

>>John Pawson, Calvin Klein, New York

>>Jigsaw, John Pawson, London, 1996
«I have certain ideas about shopping coupled with the experience I'd gained from working with Calvin Klein on the Madison Avenue shop, and one of them is a keenness for natural light whenever I can get it. I like the idea of internal vistas, and try to find the longest line, the longest possible view» (from Cliff, S., *50 Trade Secrets of Great Design Retail Spaces*, Rockport Publishers, Gloucester U.S.A. 1999).

2.4.11

REM KOOLHAAS, PRADA, NEW YORK, 2000

At the time he began working with Prada, Rem Koolhaas published a condensed anthology of essays by a number of different authors in the *Harvard Design School Guide to Shopping*[1], which gave him an opportunity to give his usual sarcastic and provocative opinions about the role, meaning and future of spaces of shopping. Starting with some remarks which have since become slogans, Rem Koolhaas laid the foundations for the concept of the *Prada Epicenters*.

His reflection on the social role of retail environments, «Shopping is perhaps the last remaining form of public activity»[2], together with the comment that everything is turning into shopping, «Not only is shopping melting into everything, but everything is melting into shopping»[3], becomes the conceptual plan for the new design project.

Shopping is such a successful parasite that it has become the host, «has infiltrated, colonized, and even replaced, almost every aspect of urban life. Town centres, suburbs, streets, and now airports, train stations, museums, hospitals, schools, the Internet, and the military are shaped by the mechanism and spaces of shopping»[4]

This dialectic allows him on the one hand to criticise the modern day deification of shopping while at the same time designing the temple of consumerism for Prada. The design, which might be described as the polar opposite of Le Corbusier's one for Bat'a, is the product of post-Fordian culture, where brand awareness depends on the level

---

[1] Chung, C. J., Inaba, J., Koolhaas, R., Leong, S. T., a cura di, *Harvard Design School Guide to Shopping*, Taschen, Köln 2001.

[2] Ibidem, p. backcover.

[3] Ibidem, p. 129.

[4] Ibidem, p. backcover.

of appeal it manages to exert. It is spectacular, serving to reverberate the image of an idea rather than to promote consumption of goods. Functions overlap in a dense ambitious functional layout where the goods are almost virtual, rarefied, in the background. Before the decision was made to commission the epicentre project to OMA and Herzog & de Meuron, Prada had no brand recognition as far as its architecture and interiors were concerned, apart from the use of a colour which in fashion circles became known as *Prada green.*

It was immediately clear that the design solution should not be one which gave an unequivocal image and that it would be the differences between the *epicenters*, that would provide the distinctive feature and continuity in the store image through the innovative use of materials, technologies and displays.

Some of the retail solutions, like using digital technology to help customers choose what to buy, turned out to be rather inefficient and purely formal. The truly innovative component was the idea of introducing cultural activities into the functional design. This was to become the crux of the design and was immediately apparent at the entrance to the shop where there was an enormous curved platform which could be used for concerts and performances. The distinctive *wave*, a continuation of the wooden flooring of the entrance which goes down the lower floor and rises up again to the first floor, is stepped on the side towards Broadway with the function of seating as well as display space. In all of this, the goods for sale are secondary, almost a detail, and the actual retail space is relegated to the rear and the basement, as well as the hanging cages in the main space.

Rem Koolhaas' radical new idea for mingling retail and cultural activities in the same space launched a series of projects on different scales. Among these, there was the Federation Square experiment in Melbourne (offices, shops, an open-air market and part of the Victoria Museum), Renzo Piano's Maison Hermès in Tokyo with a double height arcade hosting exhibitions of contemporary art, or one of the Migros premises (a Swiss supermarket chain) in Lucerne which houses a school as well as a supermarket. These have all contributed in no small way to the disappearance of a building type, the retail shop, which for so many years had been subject to such hard and fast rules.

 >>Prada Epicentre, New York, OMA, 2000

 >>Prada Beverly Hills, Los Angeles, OMA, 2004

 >>Prada Transformer, Seoul, OMA, 2009

2.4.12

REI KAWAKUBO, GUERRILLA STORES, EVERYWHERE, 2004

«It is almost easier to describe the work of Comme des Garçons in terms associated with architecture than with the traditional vocabulary of fashion»[1].

Mrs. Rei Kawakubo, Comme des Garçons' inventor, is the sole protagonist of this list of *progenitors* not coming from the architecture and design sector. In spite of this, her role in terms of project has been so influent to deserve the "Harvard Excellence in Design" Award in 2000[2]. Starting from 1973 she has redefined the limits of fashion over and over again by her radical approach always considering the project of her shops as a continuation of the project of dresses. Every shop is characterized by an original, different language. The shops were designed by either famous or young architects, always under Mrs. Kawakubo's artistic direction. The first exhibition showing her work in Italy was organized by the Sozzani Gallery in the 80's, wherein she was put near two fundamental names for the project and art culture: Franco Albini and Kris Ruhs.

The first shop which was opened in New York in 1983, based on a Takao Kawasaki's project, didn't even appear like a clothing shop. In 1998 she starts to work with Future System for opening the new space of New York in the Meat Market District: this was an area, which until that time had known nothing about any commercial structures of that type. In 2001, with Ab Rogers and Shona Kitchen, she projects a space enlivened by small red boxes moving like robots in the red, bright shop

---

[1] Brooke Hodge, Director of Exhibitions, The Graduate School of Design, Harvard University, on the occasion of the *Harvard Excellence in Design Award* given to Rei Kawakubo the 4th May 2000, at the presentation of the exhibition *Structure+Expression Comme des Garçons* at the Gund Hall Gallery May 4-31, 2000.

[2] Award of the Harvard Design School of Design.

of Faubourg Saint-Honoré in Paris, without any sign, in the second court-yard of a building.

In 2004, the results of the continuous research and experimentation and the meditation about the new market scenario as well as the customers' needs let the idea of Guerrilla Stores arise. Under the influence of unauthorized occupations (squot) by young people and underground artists, Comme des Garçons temporarily occupies the spaces found. You don't know when it will happen, you have to refer to the website, the sole information source. This is the idea, the brand does not pursue the customers, it just lets them participate by stimulating their curiosity.

In these spaces, she gathers her fashion but also the versatile research by other designers , such as the local ones, being the assistant, editor and patron of young artists.

The first Guerilla Store opens in 2004 at an ex-bookshop in Chaussestrasse at the end of the Mitte District in east-Berlin. Her collections are mixed with those from local designers and artists. She has chosen the location, then committing everything to local young designers.

Mrs. Kawakubo's intelligence and far-sightedness consisted in reprocessing and implementing processes which had raised spontaneously, acquiring their peculiar traits and developing their creative and commercial potentialities. The schizophrenic appearance and disappearance of Guerrilla Store crystallized in the Dover Street Market project of London, where, always playing ironically with the combination between establishment and provisional natural of fashion, setting and space are once again destabilized.

The diversification, the enhancement of local resources, the minimization of the concept of luxury are ways adopted by the greatest fashion brands. Even Levi's, Adidas or Prada open temporary store on the occasion of fashion or design events or small shops with an image and an idea which are diametrically opposed to that of Epicenter, Niketown or Megastores, whereby the enthusiasm for *super architecture* seems to have exploited its communication contents.

>>Comme des Garçons, Guerrilla Stores

>>Comme des Garçons Pocket

>>Comme des Garçons, New York, Future System, 1998

>>Comme des Garçons, Paris, Tadao Kawasaki, Rei Kawakubo + KRD, 2001

The shop is in a secondary street close to Faubourg Saint-Honoré, in a courtyard. KRD organizes the space that is 50 meters long and 3 wide, part for the selling and part for meditation. To get in it is necessary to get trough a red wall that opens automatically: in front there is a counter in fiberglass long as the shop. Furniture is designed by Rei Kawakubo; clothes are concentrated in the short part of the L shaped plan. Clothes are hanged in a white room on red hangers. On the other side of the courtyard there's the decompression room: when you sit on a cube, it starts moving.

>>Comme des Garçons, Dover Street Market, Londra, Tokyo, 2004-2005

Dover Street Market represents typological innovation on multi-brand store, going far from the corner concept. It hosts 12 fashion designer on six floors of the former office building. Rei Kawakubo leaves freedom to the designers to create a deliberate chaos atmosphere.

3

findings; pointers and hypothesis

3.1

findings

practice of consumption and spaces for goods

The findings of this study are summarized in a series of *Pointers*, which we have come up with rereading the *Practice of Consumption*, as well as the collection of *progenitors* in the section *The spaces for goods*; these pointers have made it possible for us to formulate some *Hypotheses* in order to understand what might constitute future guidelines for the future format of spaces of shopping.

What would seem to be clear is that we are witnessing an almost total dissolution of what the literature in the field would call the *retail building type*. Apart from its connotation of sale of goods or services, it doesn't make any sense to talk about the typology of a *shop* as the contamination with other functions and knowledge are so intense.

As our entire existence revolves around buying and exchanging goods and services, the places to which this function is allocated have changed so radically that they deserve a new more generic name such as *spaces for goods*.

From the perspective of interior design, the notions to be translated into physical space no longer concern purely functional aspects such as the sales point, display of goods or study of paths within the store, but shift to categories which bring into play broader aspects of our day to day life and which, naturally, are mirrored in our contemporary way of living.

The definition of this *potential retail* environment is changing and shifting far beyond the traditional confines of the four walls to contaminate every space, whether it be public or private. The new formats must be portable, must follow us and be prepared to occupy roles in the foreground or background depending on their physical and temporal location.

The local relevance becomes central in a context dominated by globalization. The concept of *one size fits all*, which met with enormous success between the late-60's and early-70's, is no longer suitable to satisfy different personalities. The space for commerce can no longer have the same face regardless of where it is found, whether inside a shopping centre, in a street in a historic town centre, in Rome or New Delhi. Service, the human touch, are once more becoming a catalyser in retail space. It is the only further added value needed in a world where shopping on the internet is simple, quick and cheap.

Even the world of brands which has dominated the market over the past twenty years is waking up to this change. Image, having run out of communicative appeal, needs to be replaced by content.

In the final section, *Pointers/Hypotheses*, we examine the variants and invariants of the *Practice of Consumption* and *Spaces for goods*: changes taking place in products, consumers and, consequently, places, and how these findings have in part been confirmed by recent experience, in an attempt to come up with hypotheses capable of transforming the future world of retail.

3.1.1

POINTER: THE DECLINE OF THE PRODUCT HYPOTHESIS: CURATED CONSUMPTION

«Shopping is affected by a certain predictability: for better or worse, we already know what we will find»[1].

The product, its image, the idea of its image, are no longer enough to make up for the uniformity of the what's on offer: globalization has produced a levelling of what is on offer, technology has introduced new ways of buying and the availability of products is no longer an issue because we can find what we need anywhere.

The need or want for a product is no longer enough to get me to go to a particular place.

When the object answered a material need, the shop was the place where the product made itself available. Consumer society, the widespread availability of convenience goods, advertising and marketing, have shifted most of our needs from material to immaterial necessities. The shop adapts and becomes the ideal place for representing, finding and consuming ideas, lifestyles and an imaginarium constructed ad hoc.

The crisis in the retail sector, even at the luxury goods end, is no doubt connected to the particular series of events in the world economy, but it is equally true that we have arrived at an impasse where, after the sale of products and the dreams that go with them, the shops themselves have become a product to be consumed, perhaps as mere tourists in the centre of a big city.

The dematerialization of consumption has produced a sort of implosion: the attractions which have been brought into play to mask the conceit of the intrinsic qualities of the product no longer seems to have such great

---

[1] Underhill, P., *The Call of the Mall: A Walking Tour Through the Crossroads of Our Shopping Culture*, Simon and Schuster, New York 2004, trad. it. *Antropologia dello shopping. Il fascino irresistibile dei centri commerciali*, Sperling & Kupfer, Torino 2004, p. 207.

appeal for the consumer. Research on retail space must concentrate once more on the reason it exists, that is on what it must or can sell.

Retail space, already transformed from a place for provisioning to a place for experience, contaminated with leisure and entertainment activities, seems to have exhausted its semantic value.

The practice of consumption is increasingly disassociated from material possession of goods: we wander around from shop to shop, not necessarily in order to buy things, but to find out things, a bit like the way in which people behave in libraries or museums.

The opportunity facing retail space is that of managing to combine with the world of information not as a marketing tool or to promote the product but as a system at the service of the citizen-consumer.

The increase in the availability and accessibility of information is offset by the difficulty in making choices. For the very reason that everything is available, true added value consists of knowing how to make a selection, a sort of curated consumption which relates products, services and businesses to one another.

Neither the consumption of goods not the investment of time which this requires can be relegated to a passive role. The consumer, who manages to precisely identify his requirements, needs to become part of the selection process through the acquisition of the information he needs.

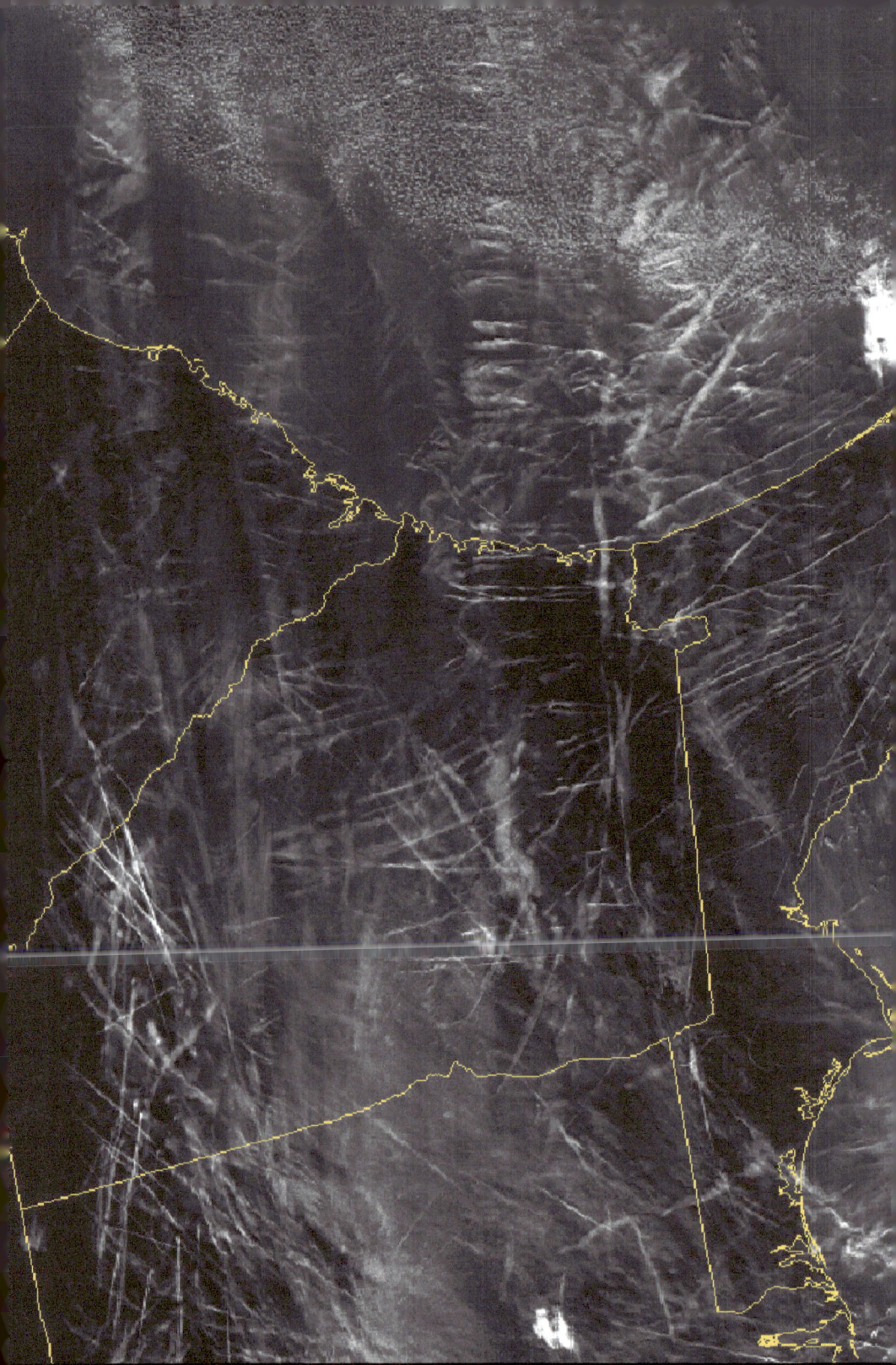

26| Contrail Clutter over Georgia.
Photo from MODIS/Terra Satellite (picture©NASA)

3.1.2

POINTER: DISAPPEARANCE OF THE TARGET
HYPOTHESIS: GENERATION C

«the shopping experience has become a representation of our normal life»[1].

A study by Carl Rodhe[2] of European and Dutch young people revealed a dissatisfaction with the parameters of the *experience economy*.

The concept of target is dissolving and the consumer, who has been surveyed, filed, and hyper-categorised no longer exists. Consumption, increasingly characterised by the ease and speed of access to information, produces an infinite number of consumer types which can no longer be classified within the bounds of rigid divisions, with consumption models which are no longer linear or easily comprehensible.

Classification according to age, gender, geographical origin, social class or purchasing power are categories which can no longer communicate information about the lifestyle of consumers. Any consideration of the role of the new space for shopping must place the consumer-user at the centre of the process, not in a passive manner, as protagonist in a pre-arranged scenario, but in an active role capable of exerting a profound influence on the economic system.

In 2005, Jeff Jarvis, the famous blogger who teaches at the school of journalism of the City University of New York, bought a computer online from Dell, a company with an excellent reputation. Unfortunately, the computer had some problems e Jarvis spent ages on the phone with the customer service without solving anything. He wrote an open letter on his blog entitled «Dell

---

[1] Van der Loo, H., *Shopping Experiences: 21st Century Cathedrals* in van Amerongen, R., Christiaans, H., *Retail & Interior Design*, Episode Publishers, Rotterdam 2004, p. 118.

[2] Carl Rohde, sociologist at Utrecht University, sociologist, is the director of the research group *Signs of the Time*; the focus of the research is how changing in social and cultural environment affect consumer's motivations.

sucks Dell lies» attracting the attention of many other bloggers and Business Week. The story had a profound and positive impact on the company which is recognised today for its highly efficient customer service «At that moment I understood that this was the beginning of the Age of the Consumer».

Consumers are increasingly involved both in the definition and generation of value, and the experience of co-creation by the consumer is transformed in that very same source of value, as Coimbatore Krishnarao Prahalad says:

> «It's the democratization of industry […] We are seeing the emergence of an economy of the people, by the people, for the people [...] Most basic change has been a shift in the role of the consumer-from isolated to connected, from unaware to informed, from passive to active»[3].

The impact of this new consumer is evident in the areas of accessibility of information, the global vision, networks, experiments and activism.

The modern day consumer is no longer happy to be an actor, but wants to feel that he is the director and screenwriter in the purchasing process, managing to go beyond the contraposition which saw the identity of the seller and buyer as separate.

In this way, a new dynamic comes into being in the relationship between producer and consumer, which involves the consumers from the production and distribution stage in the creation of the value of the goods.

>>Converse All Stars, make your own

>>Converse store in Santa Monica

---

[3] Prahalad, C. K., Ramaswamy, V., *The Future of Competition. Co-Creating Unique Value with Costumers*, Harvard Business School Press, Boston 2004.

3.1.3

POINTER: CRISIS OF THE CURRENT STORE FORMATS HYPOTHESIS: DISAPPEARANCE OF TYPOLOGY

The economic situation, ever more widespread dissent caused by the lack of social policies, dissatisfaction with environmental conditions, all these have become themes of global culture which, perhaps for the first time, finds itself involved in having to face up to the same issues.

Even in recent meetings of the powers that be of the world economy, it has emerged how the commercial sector is the one which, for better or worse, determines the prosperity and distribution of wealth around the world.

There is no questioning the capitalist system, yet there is firm intervention in the mechanisms which regulate it. An awareness of how much our purchasing choices can influence the equilibrium of the world economy together with the steady impoverishment and scarcity of natural resources have led to a state of crisis which requires us to completely rethink our lifestyle habits.

The dominant models of the spaces of commerce in terms of volume and communicative power, those of the *shopping centres* and *flagshipstores*, are feeling the impact of this crisis. Both models are in decline for the very same reasons which led to their success. As regards the *flagshipstore*, with the end of the drunken euphoria of the omnipotence of the brand, they have exhausted the imaginative repertoire they were able to generate. The mall, which arose on the back of the model of private mobility, declined as a result of the energy crisis and the impossibility of using the car because of the ubiquitous problems of traffic congestion and pollution. In the United States, there has been heated debate for some years already on the subject of how to invest in the re-use of these

practice of consumption and spaces for goods

great abandoned containers[1] and the Congress for the New Urbanism is working on creating an ecologically sustainable development model[2].

> «We have all entered the post-mall era [...] it seems that there is no future [...] we will be forced to find some way of reusing them which will release them from their present piteous condition of enormous white elephants»[3].

If modern society is characterised by differentiation and specialisation, postmodern society sees its dominant traits in contamination, the decline of linear thought and discontinuity.

In an era of convergence, through the change of habit, socio-economic conditions and political awareness, we are headed towards the disappearance of building types: this process which is certainly nothing new, has already given rise to hybrid models which are well-established by now, such as the home-office. But this trend is even more evident in the retail sector where typological contamination is so powerful as to generate new spaces where the boundary between different activities becomes ever fainter. Even the two classical building types, the residential space and the retail space are increasingly convergent with the shop, by means of modern technology, coming into the home, and the home, getting smaller in size, substituting the spaces in it once devoted to socialising with those in commercial buildings.

The energy crisis and concern about the scarcity of natural resources ensure that in recent years it has been the urban commercial centres which have experienced most growth. The users of urban centres, with

---

[1] Among the other sources:
www.deadmalls.com is mapping and photographing all the shopping centers closed and abandoned; Christensen, J., *Big Box Reuse*, MIT Press, Cambridge 2008.

[2] Tagliaventi, G., Diolaiti, D., Bucci, A., "La fine dell'era degli ipermercati: i nuovi quartieri urbani integrati" in Fumo, M., a cura di, *Dal mercato ambulante all'outlet. Luoghi e architetture per il commercio*, Editrice Compositori, Bologna 2004, p. 35.

[3] Underhill, P., *The Call of the Mall: A Walking Tour Through the Crossroads of Our Shopping Culture*, Simon and Schuster, New York 2004, trad. it. *Antropologia dello shopping. Il fascino irresistibile dei centri commerciali*, Sperling & Kupfer, Torino 2004, pp. 236-238.

a far more diversified makeup that the model of the city laid out in terms of centre versus suburbs, needs a wide and varied range of services in which the commercial component cannot prevail.

The space of commerce is the main actor of this shift, becomes a node in an open system in which goods and services concentrate about cultural hubs, places for living and working. It must be flexible and guarantee a continuous re-negotiability of its role and meaning.

There appear to me to be three development models. One the one hand, retail outlets which guarantee a high level of specialisation. If the *megastore* and *multistore* are places which can easily be replaced by virtual commerce, it will become increasingly necessary to have spaces where the customer can find a range of specific objects or services, from themed bookshops to clothes shops which sell convenient trendy outfits at reasonable prices, and food stores specialising in organic produce. At the other extreme, we will have fluid shops, characterised by the simultaneous presence of goods and services which are available to meet specific functions at different hours of the day, where the attraction is not so much the goods on sale as the variety of opportunities on offer. The third hypothesis is offered by the typical capacity of retail to assume various shapes: the *temporary shop* or *moving store* is the response to a dynamic development model and variations in the market. It occupies transition spaces, offers what the market requires at that precise moment, can expand or contract or move following market opportunities.

The general contraction in size of retail outlets can be seen in the policy adopted by the big brands who are appearing in the urban fabric in points of sale which are decidedly smaller than their flagship stores (Nike, for example, which has gone from *Niketown* to proximity stores with a high level of local relevance or to temporary stores), as well as the new policy of the large-scale retail trade. Both the retail giant Wal-Mart and the smaller supermarket chains are opening smaller stores and, in another location or inside of them, so-called *C-Stores*, convenience stores, where in the smallest possible space the shop stocks only essential goods to meet any requirement of functional shopping.

With regard to the sale of inner city space to the biggest retail chains who were practically delegated with the task of transforming the historic centres of our towns and cities into enormous open air shopping centres, differing from the cloned version of the Italian outlet village only insofar as they are built with durable materials and not plasterboard, we are faced with a development model which plans integrated urban quarters which host a mix of functions.

New design projects capable of hosting a variety of functions, in harmony with the urban fabric, can better adapt to the continuously changing city structure, with the transfer of its parts to other locations or as a result of particular economic events, by maintaining a character which can be remodelled according to the new requirements. Even if individual functions are temporarily reduced, the system maintains its capacity to grow, change and adapt.

And intervention must be aimed at a multitude of demographic groups, must include activities which can take place at different times of day, not merely adding leisure components to a retail substratum. The residential component, added to the office component to ensure dynamism on weekdays, must go side by side with cultural buildings. The reason for the success of these places need not depend on one prevailing over the others.

The form this new retail space assumes can no longer be a self-referential model but needs to *find space* in relation to the context in which it is located.

28| Albert Heijn Supermarkt, Amsterdam;
for city centre, small formats fits better

29| Mercat Santa Caterina, EMBT, 2005
One of the many covered markets recently refurbished to be transformed in specialized (food) stores.

BONGO

Bongo, Amsterdam, 2009

Bongo sells services; material goods do not exist but you can buy here an object-voucher for a romantic week-end, a massage or a dinner in a fancy restaurant.

31| Apple Store, New York, Bohlin Cywinski Jackson, 2002

Steve Jobs wanted a typology of store easily repeatable in all the stores, according to Apple image but neutral enough not to be linked to a particular Apple object. The Genius Bar, as a concept, is the most interesting innovation: «come to buy, come back to learn» is the slogan.

32| Eataly, Torino, 2007

A food supermarket with a special selection of good quality gourmet food that you can also taste in its many food stalls.

33| Dr. Martens Pop up Store, London, Campaign, 2009
Temporary Shop also for big brands.

34| Levi's Commuter, London, 2012
Not only jeans but free services for new consumers.

>>10 Corso Como, Milano, Carla Sozzani & Kris Ruhs, 1991

10 Corso Como, is the refunctionalization of few small industrial buildings in a typical Milanese court; it has been among the first to understand that the selection of products has more value than the products themselves. Apart from the traditional commercial space for clothing, and housewares, there's a bookshop, a bar, a restaurant, an art gallery and a small hotel.

>>Merci, Paris

Themed exhibitions with setting up to be sold together with the goods.

>>Ranking Ranqueen,Tokyo

Ranking Ranqueen, a Tokyo chain, sells only the top 3, 5 or 10 items in a bewildering range of categories. Rankings are based on sales data from big Tokyo department stores and independent research.

>>Supermarket, Belgrado, reMiks, 2009

On a 1400 square meters area of a former *discount*, opens Supermarket. Focus of the design were few concepts: the slow shopping, flexibility in order to organize different activities, necessity of cultural content, sustainability.

>>Vexed Generation, London, 90's

Vexed Generation, on the occasion of the London fashion week experiments a new format stores against the concept of bigness in favour of a space more intended to support cultural and political consume. The Vexed concept is abut to create counterculture of resistance against the urban condition and unfair liberal commerce, such as their clothes that helps to survive in a controversial urban context. The first shop, the White Shop in Newburgh Street opened in 1995 was a reflection over urban surveillance; a glass box, like an incubator, with little slots to see and touch clothes. A close circuit television (CCTV) was broadcasting on the outside what was happening in the inside.
The second shop in Brewick Street had the clothes connected to a compressed air machine that let them *breathe*. «Such retail spaces are far removed conceptually and physically from epicentre-style global flagship stores. Rather, they are explicitly envisaged as critical, questioning places fro consumer agency, dissident design and subversion of conventional corporate mores» (Crewe, L. *The Shopping List Compendium*, in Lee, R., Leyshon, A., McDowell, L., Sunley, P., edited by, *The Sage Companion to Economic Geography, Sage*, London 2009).

>>Bless, Berlin, Yasmine Gauster, 2004

The interior of Bless, as the dimensions of the shop, are always changing; during the summer the shop area includes also exterior space in a little garden and sometimes extend to the opposite side of the road mixing up with other shops or temporary occupying void commercial spaces.

>>5 Carlo Paveri, Pavia, Giorgi e Bonforte, 2002

The design of the space focus around the exhibition device. A very simple element puts the shop in condition to change its look, taking into consideration different type and quantity of goods.

movable retail format for special events:

>>The Gorman ShipShop, Next Architects

The Gorman ShipShop by Next Architects is a mobile retail environment that gets-up-and-goes when its market does the same.

>>Puma, Berlin, 2006

also luxury brands do experiment temporary shops:

>>Gucci Temporary store, New York

>>Temporary Chanel, Paris, 2011

One of the most contested multinational corporation, has changed lately its store policy; Nike, after Niketown, is oriented in much smaller stores where not even the name reconnects to the brand. The one in London by Wilson Brothers, is a shop but also a space for events and the meeting point of the local running club; the floor is in grind, a material by Nike made of 10% recycled runner's sole. More conventional the one in Paris, in a former library, keeps all the authentic characters with interiors design with graphics by the french Antoine + Manuel:

>>1948, London, The Wilson Brothers, 2008

>>Nike Sportswear, Paris, Antoine + Manuel, 2009

>>Bowery Stadium (Nike), Rafael de Cardenas, New York, 2010

>>Qiora, New York, Architecture Research Office, 2000
The layout of the shop of cosmetic on the Madison Avenue in New York is organized with textile walls taking in consideration the short life of the settings.

>>City Center Nijmegen, Marienburg, Joris Molenar, Vera Yanovshtchincky, 2000
A urban refunctionalization where retail plays a central role.

>>Blueprint, Droog NY, New York, Studio Makkink & Bey, 2009
Everything on sale, also the display settings for the Droog Design space in New York.

>>Eatalycoop, Bologna, Paolo Lucchetta

Eataly together with Coop Bookstore in an adaptive reuse of historical building in Bologna.

>>The Barceloneta Market

Built in the late 19th century by architect Rovira i Trias, has been rehabilitated after several years of decay.

>>Schrannenhalle Munich, Oliv Architeckten Ingenieure, 2011

Gourmet and food shop for the re-opening of the historical market.

>>Excelsior, Jean Nouvel, Milano, 2011

Luxury department store for an adaptive re-use of an old cinema in the city center of Milano.

>>Nespresso, Milano, Francis Krenpp, 2010

The decoration of the shop is directly made with the products.

the japanese fashion brand does experiment different shop format, with different scales, languages and meanings:

>>Uniqlo, Wonderwall, New York, 2011

>>Uniqlo, Lotek, New York and the States, 2006

>>Uniqlo, HWKN, New York, 2011

>>Uniqlo, Bohlin Cywinski Jackson, Shanghai, 2010

bibliography

practice of consumption and spaces for goods

A
AA. VV, *La civiltà dei superluoghi*, Damiani, Bologna 2007.
Amendola, G., *La città postmoderna. Magie e paure della metropoli contemporanea*, Laterza, Roma-Bari 1997.
Amendola, G., cura di, *La città vetrina*, Liguori Editore, Napoli 2006.
Appadurai, A., Price, P., Zinkhau, G., *The social life of things*, Cambridge University Press, Cambridge 1988.
Augé, M., *Non-lieux*, Seuil, Paris, 1992, trad. it. *Non luoghi. Introduzione a un'antropologia della surmodernità*, Elèuthera, Milano 2005.
B
Barreneche, R. A., *New Retail*, Phaidon Press, London 2005.
Barthes, R., *Mythologies*, Seuil, 1957, trad, it. *Miti d'oggi*, Einaudi, Torino 1974.
Barthes, R., *L'empire des signes*, Skira, Genève 1970, trad. it. *L'impero dei segni*, Einaudi, Torino, 1984, 1992.
Baudrillard, J., *Pour une critique de l'économie du signe*, Editions Gallimard, Paris 1972, trad. it. *Per una critica dell'economia politica del segno*, Mazzotta Editore, Milano 1974.

Baudrillard, J., *Le Système des objets*, Editions Gallimard, Paris 1968, trad. it. *Il sistema degli oggetti*, Bompiani, Milano 1972.
Baudrillard, J., *The Consumer Society*, Sage, London 1970.
Baudrillard, J., The Beaubourg Effect. Implosion and Deterrence, in Leach, N., Rethinking Architecture. A Reader in Cultural Theory, Routledge, London 1977, trad. it. *Simulacri e impostura. Bestie, Beaubourg, apparenze e altri oggetti*, Cappelli, Bologna 1980.
Bauman, Z., *Dentro la globalizzazione*, Laterza, Bari-Roma 2000.
Bauman, Z., *Modernità liquida*, Editori Laterza, Roma-Bari 2002.
Benjamin, W., *Das Passagen-Werk*, Suhrkamp, Frankfurt a. M. 1982, trad. it., *Parigi, capitale del XIX secolo. I passages di Parigi*, Einaudi, Torino 1986.
Bingham, N., *The New Boutique. Fashion and Design*,Merrel, London 2005, trad. it. *Le nuove boutique*, Idea Books, Milano 2005.
Bottini, F., *I nuovi territori del commercio. Società locale, grande distribuzione, urbanistica*, Alinea, Firenze 2005.
Bourdain, A., *La mètropole des individus*, Éditions de l'Aube, La Tour d'Aigues 2005.
Branzi, A., *Modernità debole e diffusa*, Skirà, Milano 2006.
C
Campbell, C., *The Romantic Ethic and the Spirit of Modern Consumerism*, Blackwell, Oxford 1987, trad. it *L'etica romantica e lo spirito del consumismo moderno*, Edizioni Lavoro, Roma 1992.
Cardillo, R., *Centri Commerciali naturali*, Edizioni marketing City, Modena 2005.
Cardillo, R., *Dall'associazionismo di via al marketing urbano*,Parole & Immagini, Modena 1998.
Carmagnola, F., Ferraresi, M., *Merci di culto. Ipermerce e società mediale*,Castelvecchi, Roma 1999.
Cazzullo, A., *Outlet Italia*,Mondadori, Milano 2007.
Christensen, J., *Big Box Reuse*, MIT Press, Cambridge 2008.
Chung, C. J., Inaba, J., Koolhaas, R., Leong, S. T., *Harvard Design school Guide to Shopping*, Taschen, Köln 2001.
Codeluppi, V., *La vetrinizzazione sociale*, Bollati Boringhieri, Torino 2007.
Codeluppi, V., *Lo spettacolo della merce*, Bompiani, Milano 2000.
Codeluppi, V., *I consumi: storia, tendenze, modelli*, Franco Angeli, Milano 1997.
Codeluppi, V., *Il potere del consumo. Viaggio nei processi di mercificazione della società*,Bollati Boringhieri, Torino 2003.
Codeluppi, V., *Consumo e comunicazione*, Franco Angeli, Milano 1991.
Coleman, P., *Shopping Environments*, Oxford Architectural Press, Oxfrod 2006.
D
De Certeau, M., *The Practices of Everyday Life*, Univ. California Press, Berkeley 1984, trad. it *L'invenzione del quotidiano*, Edizioni lavoro, Roma 2001.
Debord, G., *The society of Spectacle*, Zone Books, New York 1967, trad. it *La società dello spettacolo*, Baldini & Castoldi, Milano 1997.

Dell'Aria, P. V., *Architetture per il commercio*, Quaderni di architettura dell'ANCE, Roma 2005.

Derrida, J., *La voix et le phénomène. Introduction au problème du signe dans la phénoménologie de Husserl*, Presses Universitaires de France, Paris 1967, trad. it. *La voce e il fenomeno. Introduzione al problema del segno nella fenomenologia di Husserl*, Jaca Book, Milano 1968.

Desideri, P., Ilardi, M., a cura di, *Attraversamenti. I nuovi territori dello spazio pubblico*,Costa & Nolan, Genova 1997.

Desideri, P., *La città di latta. Favelas di lusso, autogrill, svincoli stradali e antenne paraboliche*, Costa & Nolan, Genova 1995.

Din, R., *New Retail*, Conran Octopus, London 2000.

F

Fabris, G., *Il nuovo consumatore verso il post-moderno*, Franco Angeli, Milano 2003.

Fabris, G., *Il consumatore post-moderno*, Franco Angeli, Milano 2005.

Fumo, M., a cura di, *Dal mercato ambulante all'outlet. Luoghi e architetture per il commercio*, Editrice Compositori, Bologna 2004.

G

Geist, J. F., *Arcades: the history of a building type*, MIT Presss, Cambridge 1985.

Gerosa, G., *Il progetto dell'identità di marca nel punto vendita*, Franco Angeli, Milano 2008.

Giddens, A., *The Consequences of Modernity*, Polity Press, Cambridge 1990, trad. It. *Le conseguenze della modernità*, Il Mulino, Bologna 1994.

Gottdiener, M., *The theming of America: dreams, visions and commercial Spaces*, Westview Press, Oxford 1997.

H

Harvey, D., *The condition of Postmodrnity*, Blackwell Pubblishing, Ames-Boston 1989, trad. it. *La crisi della modernità*, Il Saggiatore, Milano 1993.

Hawken, P., Lovins, A., Lovins, H., *Natural Capitalism. Creating the Next Industrial revolution, Little Brown & Co.*, Boston-New York-London 1999. trad. it. *Capitalismo naturale. La prossima rivoluzione industriale*, Edizioni Ambiente, Milano 1999.

Hawken, P., *The ecology of Commerce. A Declaration of Sustainability*,Harper Business, New York 1993.

I

Ilardi, M., *Negli spazi vuoti della metropoli*, Bollati Boringhieri, Torino 1999.

Ilardi, M., *La città senza luoghi*,Costa & Nolan, Genova 1990.

J

Jacobs, J., *The death and life of Great american cities*, Vintage, New York 1961.

K

Klanten, R., K. Bolhöfer, *Out of the Box!*, Germany 2011.

Klein, N., *No logo*, Knopf Canada, Toronto 2000, trad. it. Baldini e Castoldi, Milano 2002.

L

La Cecla, F., *Contro l'architettura*,Bollati Boringhieri, Torino 2008.

Lanzani, A., *I paesaggi italiani*, Meltemi, Roma 2003.

Lash, S., Urry, J., *Economies of Signs and Space*, Sage, London 1994.

Levinson, J. C., *Guerrilla Marketing*, Houghton Mifflin, Boston 1993.

M

Maldonado, T., *Reale e virtuale*, Feltrinelli, Milano 1992.

Manuelli, S., *Design for shopping*, Laurence King Publishing, London 2006, trad. it.*Negozi di tendenza*, Logos, Modena 2006.

Manzini, E., Jégiu, F., *Quotidiano sotenibile. Scenari di vita urbana*, Edizioni Ambiente, Milano 2003.

Marenco Mores, C., *From Fiorucci to the Guerrilla stores: shop displays in architecture, marketing and communications*, Marsilio-Fondazione Pitti Discovery, Venezia 2006, trad. it. *Da Fiorucci ai Guerrilla Stores*, Marsilio, Venezia 2006.

P

Pevsner, N., *A History of Building types*, Princeton Architectural Press, New York 1976, trad. it. *Storia e caratteri degli edifici*, Fratelli Palombi Editori, Roma 1986.

Pine, J., Gilmore, H., *The Experience Economy*, Harvard Business School Press, Boston 1999, trad. it. *L'economia delle esperienze: oltre il servizio*, Etas, Milano 2000.

Plunkett, D. , Reid, O., *Detail in Contemporary Retail Design*, Laurence King Publishing, United Kingdom 2012.

R

Rifkin, J. C., *The Age of Access. The New Culture of Hypercapitalism where all of Life is a Paid-for Experience,* Penguin Putman Inc., New York 2000, trad. it. *L'era dell'accesso. La rivoluzione della new economy,* Mondadori, Milano 2002.

Ritzer, G., *La religione dei consumi, cattedrali, pellegrinaggi e riti dell'iperconsumismo,* Il Mulino, Bologna 2000.

Ritzer, G., *The McDonaldization Thesis: Explorations and* Extensions, Sage, London 1998.

Ritzer, G., *Enchanting a Disenchanted World: Revolutionizing the Means of Consumption,* Pine Forge Press, London-New Delhi 1999, trad. it *La religione dei consumi,*Il Mulino, Bologna 1999.

Ritzer, G., *The mcDonaldisation of society,* Pine Forse Press, London 1996, trad. it. *Il mondo alla Mc Donald's,*Il Mulino, Bologna 1996.

Rudofsky, B., *Strade per la gente. Architettura e ambiente umano,* Laterza, Bari 1981.

S

Schmitt, B., Ferraresi, M., *Experiential marketing,* Free Press, New York 1999. trad. it.*Marketing esperienziale: come sviluppare l'esperienza di consumo,* Franco Angeli, Milano 2006.

Scodeller, D., *Negozi. L'architetto nello spazio della merce,* Electa, Milano 2007.

Scott Brown, D., Venturi, R., *Learning from Las Vegas,* MIT Press, Cambridge 1972, trad. it. *Imparando da Las Vegas,* Ed. Cluva, Venezia 1985.

Smiley, D. J., *Sprawl and Public Space: Redressing the Mall,* National Endowment for the Arts, Washington 2002.

Sorkin, M., *Variations on a Theme Park: The New American City and the End of Public Space,* Hill and Wang, New York 1992.

Sorkin, M., "Brand Aid. Or, the Lexus and the Guggenheim (Further tales of the Notorious B.I.G.ness)", *Harvard Design Magazine,* n. 17, Autumn 2002-Winter2003.

Sudjic, D.,"Breve storia dello shopping", *Fashion,*allegato a *Domus,* n. 858, 2003.

U

Underhill, P., *The Call of the Mall: A Walking Tour Through the Crossroads of Our Shopping Culture,* Simon and Schuster, New York 2004, trad. it. *Antropologia dello shopping. Il fascino irresistibile dei centri commerciali,* Sperling & Kupfer, Torino 2004.

Underhill, P., *Why we buy,* Simon & Schuster, New York 1999.

V

Van Amerongen, R., Christiaans, H., *RETAIL & INTERIOR DESIGN,* Episode Publishers, Rotterdam 2004.

Vernet, D., de Wit, L., *Boutiques and Other Retail Spaces* , Routledge, London 2007.

Z

Zardini, M., a cura di, *Paesaggi ibridi. Un viaggio nella città contemporanea,* Skirà, Milano 1996.

Zukin, S., *Point of purchase.How shopping changed american culture,* Routledge, London 2004.

ABOUT THE AUTHOR

Francesca Murialdo, architect and European PhD in Interior Architecture and Exhibition Design at Politecnico di Milano, lives in Milano.
From 1998 she collaborates with the School of Architecture and School of Design of Politecnico di Milano as researcher, supervisor, professor, both in Italy than abroad.
From 2006 research has been focused on Retail Design with academic courses at the School of Design, Politecnico di Milano (http://laboworks.org/)
laboMint is the professional side that from Milano is networking dealing with interior design and concept design both as strategic consultant and professional practice, both for Italian and international spaces.

More detail on
www.labomint.com

www.ingramcontent.com/pod-product-compliance
Lightning Source LLC
Chambersburg PA
CBHW040132270326
41929CB00005B/33